Ontology-Based
Evolution of
Domain-Oriented
Languages

Eduard Babkin • Boris Ulitin

Ontology-Based Evolution of Domain-Oriented Languages

Models, Methods and Tools for
User Interface Design in
General-Purpose Software Systems

Eduard Babkin (iD)
HSE University
Nizhny Novgorod, Russia

Boris Ulitin (iD)
HSE University
Nizhny Novgorod, Russia

ISBN 978-3-031-42201-0   ISBN 978-3-031-42202-7   (eBook)
https://doi.org/10.1007/978-3-031-42202-7

This Springer imprint is published by the registered company Springer Nature Switzerland AG
The registered company address is: Gewerbestrasse 11, 6330 Cham, Switzerland

Paper in this product is recyclable.

Preface

This work focuses on the notion of domain-specific languages (DSLs) in the context of modelling the structure of interfaces of general-purpose software systems. In this case, the structure refers to the set of objects involved in an interface and the relationships between them. Algorithmic DSLs used to describe the solution of some problem within a domain are not the focus of this book. It is important to note that the DSL approaches used in this work are applicable to the modelling of both software interfaces between the various components of a complex software system and human-machine interfaces (i.e., objects and links displayed on the screen and used by the user). Within the scope of this study, we demonstrate the application and development of these approaches only to improve the efficiency of human-machine interface design as part of general-purpose software systems.

Domain-oriented programming has one main principle. And the principle says that you should always focus on a single mission, for which a specific, specialized programming language has been developed, which is used just to solve this set mission better than all known methods. DSLs are used in a narrow domain, taking into account all its specific points. Their main task is to solve all the problems of the application for which they were created. Therefore, domain-oriented programming is a rather specific area of development. It is tied around some specific activity and with some unique language. In fact, there are a lot of such "microspheres" where a separate DSL is used. In general, domain-specific programming touches areas where general-purpose languages cannot "reach" or where their use is simply inappropriate. Very often, a DSL is used as an addition to the main programming languages, expanding their capabilities and sphere of influence.

It is difficult to define the advantages and disadvantages of a DSL, if only because it functions in very specific domains where it simply would not work out "in a different way." This is the same as evaluating the merits of surgery or dentistry as a field of medicine. On the other hand, like any language, DSLs have similar components in their structure (its semantics and syntax). In addition, based on the domain, the DSL must conform to the domain model. Consequently, we can "dissect" the DSL at the level of objects and relationships by establishing a correspondence between the DSM and the DSL.

This correspondence opens up great opportunities for using various model-based approaches to the development of DSLs. It is these ideas that form the basis of our study and the proposed projection approach to the development of DSLs. The main goal of this study is to demonstrate the possibilities of the projection approach and its flexibility in the context of the DSL evolution. In our case, we use the ontological representation as the initial domain model. This is reasonable both from the point of view of the model-oriented approach (the ontology is a formal artifact and can be used in cross-model transformations) and from the point of view of universality (there are a large number of ontologies with varying degrees of domain detail). In addition, ontologies contain not only a set of objects and relationships between them but also domain constraints, which are essential and must be taken into account in the case of developing domain-specific languages.

Our results are presented in the following form. The introduction (Chap. 1) presents the relevance of the work, the aim and objectives of the research, the scientific novelty, and the theoretical and practical significance of the research, as well as a summary of the contents of the work.

Chapter 2 analyzes the existing classical DSL design and implementation methodology for modelling general-purpose human-machine interfaces in the context of the life cycle of general-purpose software systems. For this purpose, the chapter provides the definition of a DSL and its place in general-purpose software systems. A description of the main stages of the classical life cycle of DSLs and software systems is presented. The shortcomings of existing DSL lifecycle management methods for modelling human-machine interfaces of general-purpose software systems are highlighted.

Based on this analysis, it is concluded that the life cycles of DSLs and general-purpose software systems are not fully consistent. As a consequence, there is a need to develop methods that not only address the shortcomings of the classical approach to software development for modelling general-purpose human-machine interface software systems but also support its evolution in line with the evolution of the subject domain.

Chapter 3 is devoted to an analysis of existing methods and formalisms used in describing the structure of a DSL for modelling general-purpose human-machine interfaces of software systems. In particular, formalizations of artifacts, such as domain semantic model (DSM) and the components of DSL structure, semantics, abstract, and concrete syntax, are considered.

Based on the analysis of classical approaches to the formalization of a DSL for the modeling of general-purpose human-machine interfaces of software systems, a generalized unified model-oriented representation of a DSL for the modeling of general-purpose human-machine interfaces of software systems is formulated. This representation makes it possible to represent each component of the DSL structure as a model and the DSL evolution process as a set of cross-model transformations.

Formation of such a unified representation makes it possible to directly use the results of subject domain analysis (its representation in the form of a DSM) in the process of DSL development for general-purpose software systems' human-machine interface modeling, thereby automating the processes of DSL structure determination, thus eliminating the need for DSL re-creation in case of DSM modification in the process of subject domain evolution.

Chapter 4 provides a detailed description of the proposed new projection-based approach to the development of DSLs for modelling human-machine interfaces of general-purpose software systems, based on the model-based representation of the DSL structure formulated in the previous chapter. In the proposed projection approach, the transition between the different components of the DSL structure takes place by applying a set of cross-model transformation rules that ensure not only that changes made in the DSL are consistent with changes in the subject domain (DSM) but also that the DSL evolution process can be automated.

The resulting set of cross-model transformation rules for organizing DSL evolution based on graph transformations can be applied to DSL design for modelling general-purpose DSLs of software systems in various subject areas. For this purpose, only parts of the rules need to be adapted according to the used subject domain models, while the structure of the rules and their set remain unchanged.

Based on this set of cross-model transformation rules, the chapter presents details of the algorithmization and software implementation of the human-machine interface evolution procedure for general-purpose software systems. The software algorithms developed have been used to implement software systems in the two subject areas described in the next chapter.

Chapter 5 describes and analyzes the software implementation of the human-machine interface evolution of general-purpose software systems as an example of an external DSL in two subject domains: "Software System for University Admissions Office" and "Software System for Resource Allocation of Railway Station." The definition of cross-model transformation rules in ATL language is presented [7] to implement the horizontal and vertical evolution of a DSL for modelling human-machine interfaces of general-purpose software systems. Tools (modules) are developed to support DSL evolution for simulation of general-purpose human-machine interfaces of software systems. The results of the evaluation of the characteristics of existing and proposed software environments are given according to the following criteria: time to modify the DSL and number of lines of code manually inserted during the DSL modification.

Chapter 6 is devoted to the analysis of the subsequent application of the proposed projection approach for more complex systems, namely, decision support systems based on heterogeneous information of decision-makers. In this case, we demonstrate the possibilities of the approach for implementing evolution both at the level of the DSL and the original DSM (a set of criteria and their limitations, adapted to each expert participating in the assessment).

The conclusion (Chap. 7) of the work contains a list of the main results of the research, an assessment of the level of achievement of the objective, as well as suggestions for the further development and practical application of the findings in various subject domains.

Nizhny Novgorod, Russia   Eduard Babkin
June 2023   Boris Ulitin

Acknowledgments

I would like to express my sincere gratitude to Tatiana, whose continuous support and benevolent patience became a solid foundation of my scientific endeavors.

Nizhny Novgorod, Russia   Eduard Babkin

Foremost, I would like to express my sincere gratitude to my advisor Prof. Eduard Babkin for the continuous support of my PhD study and research, for his patience, motivation, enthusiasm, and immense knowledge. His guidance helped me all the time in the research and writing of this thesis. I could not have imagined having a better advisor and mentor for my PhD study.

Besides my advisor, I would like to thank my thesis committee, Prof. Sergey Zykov, Prof. Abdulrab S. Habib, Prof. Robert Pergl, Dr. Sergey Shershakov, and Dr. Rostislav Yavorskiy, for their encouragement, insightful comments, and hard questions.

Last but not the least, I would like to thank my family for giving birth to me in the first place and supporting me throughout my life.

Nizhny Novgorod, Russia   Boris Ulitin

The research is supported by grant of the RSF (project № 23-21-00112 "Models and methods to support sustainable development of socio-technical systems in digital transformation under crisis conditions").

Contents

Acronyms

ADSL	Algorithmic Domain-Specific Language
DPD	Digital Product Development
DSL	Domain-Specific Language
DSM	Domain-Semantic Model
GTS	Graph Transformation System
LTS	Labeled Transition System
M2M	Model-To-Model (e.g., M2M transformation)
MCC	Minimal Constructive Component
MCU	Minimal Constructive Unit
MDSL	Modelling Domain-Specific Language
NAC	Negative Application Condition
OWL	Web Ontology Language
PAC	Positive Application Condition
PDSL	Programming Domain-Specific Language
SS/SwS	Software System
TGG	Triple Graph Grammar

Chapter 1
Research Background

Abstract To begin with, we present the prerequisites for this study, i.e. its scientific and practical background. Such an initial immersion in the subject of the study will allow a more complete presentation of the concepts described in the future, as well as compose a single conceptual apparatus. We also specify the context of the study and its main goals and research methods.

Relevance of the Topic

From a computer science point of view, a DSL is a computer language (including programming or modeling) with limited expressive power, oriented toward a specific subject domain [36]. From a more general point of view (including the linguistic aspects of DSL as a language), a DSL is an artificial language which semantically and syntactically conforms to some domain of interest [45].

Often, the DSL is developed as part of some more general software system (which is referred to as the core system in relation to the DSL). In this sense, the DSL is related to the general-purpose language used in building the underlying system and, in relation to it, may be internal or external [36].

Internal DSLs are written in the language of the main application and are embedded in that language [36]. From this point of view, internal DSLs represent a specific way of using the general-purpose language used in the creation of the main application. As a consequence, approaches specific to general-purpose languages are applicable to the development of internal DSLs, and their analysis is beyond the scope of this study.

Unlike internal DSLs, external DSLs are written separately from the main system. Once created, such languages are embedded in the main application as a compiler or interpreter [36]. The main advantage of external DSLs is that they can better reflect the concepts of the subject area and the requirements of the customer [98].

For the purposes of this work, we consider only external DSLs used for modeling general-purpose software system interfaces. This is efficient and justified from the point of view that the human-machine interface of software systems has limited functionality (directly related to the functionality of the system as a whole), as do

DSLs, and can in this sense be considered as a special kind of DSL [61]. It is for this reason that the incorporation of DSL design and modification elements into the design and modification of software systems can be effective and provide greater flexibility for the latter with respect to the requirements of different categories of users [25].

There is interest in DSL among researchers and practitioners alike [61, 72]. First and foremost, this is due to the fact that DSLs are a convenient, comprehensible, and sufficiently user-friendly mechanism for managing the subject area for which they are created [36].

Research on the problems of developing DSLs has been devoted to the work of many domestic scientists, in particular I.S. Anureyev [79], B.N. Gaifullin and V.E. Tumanov [45], A.O. Sukhov [98], V.G. Fedorenkov and P.V. Balakshin [34], etc. This topic is also reflected in the works of foreign scholars such as Pablo Gómez-Abajo, Esther Guerra, Juan de Lara [41], Aleksandar Popovic, Ivan Lukovic, Vladimir Dimitrieski, Verislav Djuki [85], Walter Cazzola, Edoardo Vacchi, etc.

In addition, a large number of works are devoted to studies in related fields, in particular, the definition and dynamics of semantics are explored in the works of A.P. Ershov [32], L.A. Kalinichenko [59, 115], Guizzardi [43, 44], Stoy [97], Strachey [75], etc., and the definition of the syntactic aspects of a DSL is explored in the works of Evans [33], Laird [64], etc.

In most modern studies [36, 61, 82], the process of DSL development includes the following steps: decision-making (whether the DSL should be created, in other words, a feasibility study), analysis of the subject area (for which the DSL is created), DSL design (which includes defining the whole DSL structure and choosing the most appropriate type of DSL), DSL implementation, and deployment of the DSL.

Also, it is sometimes seen as a separate stage of DSL support (which includes the possibility of DSL evolution) [24]. Evolution can occur as a consequence of changes in the domain itself [24, 25] and also be influenced by internal factors, such as changes in the behavior of system users [64] and their heterogeneity [83].

However, as the analysis of the publications shows, the works do not cover the mechanism of tracking changes in the domain and translating them to the DSL model. Moreover, it is believed that by the time the DSL is developed, the domain model itself has already been manually transferred to the DSL model (as, e.g., in papers [41, 54]). It is fair to say that a number of researchers, including Peter Bell [10], Josh G.M. Mengerink, Alexander Serebrenik, Mark van den Brand [69], Ramon R.H. Schiffelers [70], and in particular Jonathan Sprinkle and Gabor Karsai [94], investigate the issue of evolution of graphical models of the domain. But they do not consider the consequent transfer of changes made to models and their supporting rules to DSL models [94]. On the contrary, these authors try to keep the DSL structure unchanged, which is inconsistent with the assumption that the DSL model is identical to the domain model, which means that any change in the domain model should result in an equivalent change in the DSL model.

The question of DSL evolution is even more relevant in the case of DSLs for modeling general-purpose human-machine interfaces of software systems, since the lifecycle of software systems implies a support phase of the software system, implying its development (modification) to meet new user requirements [64].

To emphasize the importance of this requirement, the work uses the notion of a dynamic context in which the support phase of a software system takes place. The dynamic context is understood in this chapter as a set of changing models of the subject area and/or a set of competencies of users. The existence of a dynamic context necessitates the adaptation of software system interfaces to new user requirements, as well as in accordance with changes in the models of the domain for which the software system is created [25].

As a consequence, changes to the system must be reflected in the DSL, which also exists in a dynamic context. However, in the DSL lifecycle, the maintenance phase is optional, and the existing DSL development tools do not support the functionality to organize the full evolution of the DSL [61]. As a consequence, efficiency problems can arise in the use of a DSL-based software system [24].

In this context, the task of proposing approaches, methods, and tools to support the evolution of the DSL for modeling human-machine interfaces of general-purpose software systems is relevant.

The aim of the study is to improve the efficiency of lifecycle support processes for general-purpose software systems by developing new models and methods for the evolution of DSLs for modeling interfaces.

Criteria in accordance with ISO 25010-2015 shall be used to assess performance [47], including software modification time, number of manually inserted lines of code to modify interfaces, etc.

Research Methods

In what follows we use formal mathematical methods such as function theory, graph theory [94], graph grammars [19], and elements of predicate logic [31]; UML diagrams and conceptual (semantic) models in the form of codified ontologies [51] and object-relational models [19].

The practical part of the work applies compilation methods, declarative tools for transformations on graphs [13], and object-oriented and event-driven programming methods.

Scientific Novelty

Based on the analysis of existing approaches and methods for DSL development, a generalized model-oriented DSL structure, which is a unified representation of all levels of DSL structure, is presented.

Different types (models) of DSL evolution are formalized for modeling the human-machine interface for general-purpose software systems, allowing the consistent evolution of the DSM and all DSL levels to be defined according to the proposed projection approach.

A set of cross-model transformations (based on graph transformations) is constructed and implemented to organize the horizontal and vertical evolution of the external modeling DSL of general-purpose software system interfaces.

On the basis of the selected set of cross-model transformations, a new method (called the projection approach) is proposed for the development of an external

DSL for the modeling of general-purpose human-machine interfaces of software systems. The proposed projection approach allows to automate the process of DSL development for modeling general-purpose software interfaces and to use the results of subject domain analysis (its representation in the form of DSM) in DSL design and implementation, as well as to organize the automated evolution of DSL.

In accordance with the proposed method, an algorithmization and software implementation of the transformation procedure as an example of an external DSL for modeling the DSL of general-purpose software systems for two subject domains has been carried out.

The analysis of the performed software implementation of the transformation procedure as an example of an external DSL revealed reusable results. On this basis, it is concluded that the proposed approach and models of DSL evolution are applicable for DSL evolution implementation in various subject domains and are the basis for developing universal software tools to support the full DSL lifecycle (including the DSL evolution phase).

Practical Value of the Results
The study developed a new engineering method (projection approach) to develop an external DSL for general-purpose software system interface modeling to improve the efficiency and convenience of DSL evolution support processes for general-purpose software system human-machine interface modeling. In support of the proposed approach, the algorithmization and software implementation of the human-machine interface transformation procedure was performed as an example of an external DSL.

The prototypes of software environments using the proposed DSL-based projection approach (with evolution capabilities in dynamic contexts) for the subject domains "Admission Committee Software System" and "Railway Station Resource Allocation Software System" were implemented (Java language and Eclipse plug-ins were used for development; total number of code lines of both prototypes—22,483). The developed prototypes allow not only to execute scenarios on the DSL but also to modify the structure of all DSL levels in real time without having to re-create the DSL and the software systems as a whole.

The experience of operating the developed software prototypes has shown that their use minimizes the number of errors and conflicts during the modification (evolution) of the DSL and the software environment as a whole, since all changes to the DSL are made in an automated form, without the need for manual modification. As a consequence, the total time required to modify the DSL and the software environment as a whole is also reduced.

The proposed approach to support the evolution of DSLs for modeling general-purpose software system interfaces is applicable to the implementation of general-purpose software environments of various subject areas with dynamic contexts of use, in particular in highly adaptive areas such as so-called smart systems and cyber-physical systems [61].

Part I
The Place of a Domain-Specific Language in Modern Information Systems

Chapter 2
Analysis of Approaches to the Development of a DSL for Software Systems

Abstract Before talking about the proposed new approach to the development of DSLs, it is necessary to analyze the existing theoretical and practical experience of existing examples of DSLs. This chapter analyzes existing classical approaches to the design and development of DSLs on the basis of the current scientific literature. In addition, the section provides an analysis of the use of DSL in the context of the development of more general information systems.

2.1 Definition, Classification, and General Structure of the DSL

A domain-specific language (DSL) is a computer language created for a specific domain [36]. From this point of view, a DSL formalizes within itself the structure, behavior, as well as the constraints and requirements of a given domain. Unlike general-purpose languages that are not strictly domain-specific, DSLs have limited expressiveness and provide support only for the upper level of domain abstraction [10]. As a consequence, DSLs actually contain within themselves some model of the domain, thereby allowing users to operate with terms and concepts of the domain. Furthermore, in DSLs, it is also possible to take subject matter boundaries into account, thus excluding incorrect expressions in the DSL [24].

It is important to note that the way in which the constraints of the domain will be taken into account depends on the type of DSL to be developed. Most commonly, DSLs are used as part of a software system (called a core system) that uses a general-purpose language to create it. In relation to a given general-purpose language, DSLs may be of two kinds: internal and external [36].

Internal DSLs are written in and embedded in the general-purpose language used to build the core system [36]. From this point of view, internal DSLs represent a specific way of using a general-purpose language, and thus, the approaches used for general-purpose languages are applicable for the development and subsequent evolution of such DSLs.

© The Author(s), under exclusive license to Springer Nature Switzerland AG 2024
E. Babkin, B. Ulitin, *Ontology-Based Evolution of Domain-Oriented Languages*,
https://doi.org/10.1007/978-3-031-42202-7_2

7

In contrast to internal DSLs, external ones are those that are written separately from the main (core) system. Once created, they are embedded in the host application as a compiler or interpreter. The main advantage of external DSLs is that they can best reflect the concepts of the domain and the requirements of the customer (or end user) [98]. As a consequence, when working with external DSLs, users operate with terms that are familiar to them in the domain.

In addition, depending on the purpose for which they are used, DSLs can be divided into programming DSLs (PDSLs) and modeling DSLs (MDSLs) [98]. MDSLs are used as part of the process of developing domain-specific models (e.g., human-machine interface languages) [54], while PDSLs are used by humans to state a task to a computer (e.g., SQL) [36] and are structurally identical to modern programming languages [61]. In what follows, we will only consider external DSL software for modeling human-machine interfaces.

In addition, it should be noted that in terms of the format in which language constructions are presented, external DSLs can be divided into textual and visual ones [98]. However, this division in this case is conditioned only by the final representation (visualization) of language constructions (in text form or in graphic form, as icons) for an end user and does not depend in any way on the form in which these constructions are set at the level of the DSL structure.

This is why, in what follows, we will consider the structure of a DSL in its most general form, formulating statements that are the same for any DSL, regardless of its type. This is also reasonable from the point of view that the structure of a DSL (as of any language) contains semantic and syntactic components [44]. Semantics of the language is fully determined by a conceptual (semantic) model of the domain, giving a meaning to the syntactic components, thus guaranteeing the coherence of the whole DSL with the domain [43]. Abstract syntax defines a set of objects that are present and can be used in the language, thus being a certain projection of the semantic component of the language [98]. Concrete syntax in this case expresses the actual designations for the objects of the abstract syntax and identifies the ways to define them in terms of a concrete language [5]. This division of the DSL syntax into abstract and concrete is fully consistent with the assumption that several DSLs can be created for a single target domain and that different dialects of the same DSL can use the same abstract model of the target domain, defining only different concrete syntax commands to operate on it.

2.2 DSL Lifecycle Models

In most modern studies [36, 61, 82], the process of DSL development includes the following stages: decision-making (on the need for the DSL, in other words, its applicability analysis), analysis of the domain (for which the DSL is being created), DSL design (which includes defining the whole DSL structure and choosing the most appropriate type of DSL), DSL implementation, and deployment of the DSL.

Fig. 2.1 The classic DSL lifecycle

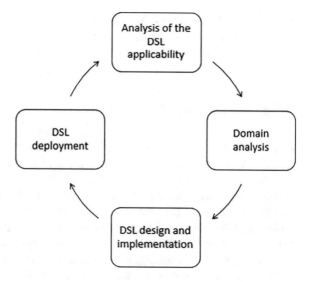

It is also sometimes seen as a separate phase of DSL support (which includes the possibility of DSL evolution) [24].

Note that in this case (Fig. 2.1) it does not matter whether the DSL is textual or graphical (visual), as the differences between these types of DSL become significant only at the stage of direct implementation of the DSL. A more detailed analysis of the differences between the two types of DSL can be found in the paper by A. Sukhov [98].

2.2.1   Analysis of the Applicability of the DSL

This stage is, from some points of view, the most important stage in deciding to develop a domain-specific solution. At this stage, the designer has only the formulation of the initial problem to which the object-oriented approach can be applied (among others). The outcome of this stage is a decision on the feasibility and effectiveness of the approach. Among all the factors that can influence the final decision on the development of the DSL, the main ones are [10]:

- Having a sufficiently narrow subject area and having recurrent tasks within it.
- Experience in the subject area.
- The development team has experience in creating subject-oriented solutions using a variety of tools.
- Interest and resources from end users (customers).

As can be seen from all of the above, the applicability analysis phase of the DSL mainly involves interaction between end users and system developers. This interaction implies an expert assessment of the domain in general and the individual task within it in particular. As a consequence, the decision on the feasibility of a domain-specific solution is based on the developers' own experience and poorly formatted knowledge of the domain and cannot be fully automated.

2.2.2   Domain Analysis

First of all, this phase is devoted to a detailed analysis and decomposition of the domain. As the name implies, the main result of this phase of work on the DSL is the construction of a semantic model of the domain (based on expert experience), containing the main entities (concepts and their attributes) for the future DSL and the relationships between them. In addition to the resulting model, a domain dictionary (glossary), including possible names for each individual entity, can be compiled. This will make the language to be developed more flexible and customize it according to the terminology of each individual user group.

Domain analysis can be conducted using both formal methodologies, in particular DARE (Domain Analysis and Reuse Environment) [94] and FODA (Feature-Oriented Domain Analysis) [107], and with the help of other (informal) methods (for a more detailed analysis of such methods, see [68, 72]). It should be noted that, in this case, the methods are universal in the context of different types of DSL, both textual and visual, as the approaches used for the analysis of the target domain are practically independent of the subsequent implementation of the DSL. The following artifacts may be used as a basis for analyzing the domain [72].

- Some existing library that performs the functions to be implemented in a future DSL. In this case, language concepts can be taken directly from existing code.
- Interviewing domain experts in order to identify their means of expressing knowledge of the domain (so-called professional language)—frequently used designations can form the basis for the semantic level of the future DSL.
- If there is already some information system in use within the domain, its interface can be a good source of entities for the future DSL.

Unfortunately, as noted by the authors [72], the existing software tools for DSL development do not support the functionality to perform domain analysis. This limitation is primarily a consequence of the limitations imposed on domain analysis tools by the methodology used (e.g., when using FODA, a visual language for describing requirements is required [107], while a conventional UML or ER diagram is sufficient for expert knowledge analysis). As a consequence, specialized knowledge engineering tools are more frequently used in practice.

The introduction of such tools into DSL development platforms is seen as useful because it can greatly facilitate and streamline the process of assembling the subject matter entities that form the basis of the semantics of a future DSL. In addition, the introduction of such tools would make the work on DSLs more flexible by allowing the reuse of already defined domain entities and the creation of a consistent DSL dialect tree instead of a multitude of disjointed DSLs for individual tasks.

Furthermore, the results of the domain analysis, expressed in the form of a semantic model, can be used as a prototype metamodel for a future DSL and apply cross-model transformations (and other model transformation techniques) to generate the latter, thereby making it possible to track how changes in domain knowledge will affect the metamodel and to organize the evolution of the DSL while maintaining its coherence with the domain.

2.2.3 Design and Implementation of the DSL

The design and implementation of a DSL are the most studied stages of the DSL lifecycle and are supported by all existing DSL development platforms. In addition to the description of the language itself, these stages also include the development of related tools for working with the DSL both at the stage of its implementation and at the stage of future use: language editor (visual or textual), generator (DSL scripts), domain-specific library, etc. (the whole set of possible tools is described in detail in [54]). It is important to note that from this phase onward, the differences between the different types of DSL become apparent and significant, since textual languages are usually defined by means of grammars and visual languages by means of metamodels.

Usually, the activities of designing and implementing a DSL include formalizing the abstract syntax of the language to be created (most often in the form of a metamodel), defining the specific syntax, automatically generating a language editor from these descriptions, and describing (in one form or another) the semantics of the language [61]. As a rule, in this case, the denotational semantics is specified [97] by creating a generator from the models in the visual language into some textual language. However, it is also possible to specify rules for interpreting DSLs (e.g., in the form of operational semantics [116] in the form of a set of model transformation rules).

A separate issue that needs to be mentioned, which is often neglected in works on visual DSLs but often mentioned in articles on textual DSLs, is the question of reusing the syntax of already created DSLs. At first sight, this question seems to be relevant only for textual languages; however, as shown in [64], this issue is relevant for both types of DSLs, since when implementing any type of DSL, it is possible to use already existing languages as a base for the one being created, either by creating various extensions (e.g., using the UML profile mechanism) or by reusing and extending parts of existing metamodels.

However, existing technologies for the most part do not support this trend and force the user to create the DSL from scratch (the exception is MetaEdit+ [74] and XTend [29], but they have limited or no functionality to create a specific DSL syntax and therefore also have this limitation). In order to support full reuse of metamodels, tools need to incorporate special tools that allow the transformation of different metamodels with the possibility of their subsequent decomposition and/or import.

2.2.4   Deployment of the DSL

The DSL deployment phase involves language support tools that need to be installed on end user workstations (who also need to be trained in the use of these tools) [64]. In the case of a DSL, the preparation of the installation and configuration of the tools is not particularly difficult. The focus is on working with users.

Although DSLs are created specifically for the convenience and knowledge of specific groups of end users, there are peculiarities in the acceptance of DSL concepts and the need to develop a habit of working with them [67]. This is because, firstly, people are used to using existing software environments and, secondly, DSLs will almost always be new to users. As a consequence, there is a psychological rejection of the need to learn a DSL applicable to a narrow field, the knowledge of which will not increase the value of employees in the labor market.

However, it is important to note that, given the specifics of DSL development and its syntax, based on a semantic model of the domain, the learning process should be as easy as possible for end users and not require special training. Otherwise, a DSL loses its advantages over any other software tools. Ideally, a DSL should support the ability to make changes on user demand, i.e., support evolution. However, this feature of the DSL is not implemented in existing DSL systems and, as mentioned earlier, any change to the DSL actually results in the creation of a new DSL.

2.2.5   Shortcomings of Existing DSL Lifecycle Management Methods to Support DSL Evolution

As shown above, the DSL lifecycle, although it contains all the stages necessary for the implementation of the DSL, is insufficiently explored with regard to the implementation of the evolution of the DSL.

In the process of using the created DSL, users have a lot of comments and suggestions. This is due, on the one hand, to the fact that both the domain and the set of end user tasks may change over time [68]. Usually, both of these factors lead to new requirements for the DSL which have to be implemented in the new version of the DSL in order to meet the updates in both the domain and the requirements of the users [83]. However, this important phase of the lifecycle is often simply ignored by researchers and authors of DSL tools.

The availability of tools to support the evolution phase of the DSL is essential for any DSL development platform that is to be used in industrial projects. This is primarily due to the fact that users must not lose the results of their work: regardless of changes in the language and/or its metamodel, all previously created artifacts must continue to be opened in the editor [25].

Several approaches can be used to support such compatibility between new models and previously implemented models. For example, metamodels can be extended to include information about the version of the metamodel with which they were created, and converters can be created manually to convert models to newer versions. Such converters can be based on a model conversion tool (e.g., Eclipse Modeling Project [29]—model migration rules are described as cross-model (model-to-model, M2M) conversions. This approach is extremely common in text-based development environments (IDEs) that support the functionality of converting a project created in an earlier version of the IDE to the current version.

Another alternative to support the compatibility of new models with previously implemented models is to use automated model migration tools (based on information about differences between metamodel versions). However, this approach also requires manual handling of various conflicts that arise during model migration (e.g., if the type of an attribute has changed from string to numeric and the value of the original model cannot be converted to numeric format, the user has to set the new value of the corresponding attribute manually). In such cases, the new version of the editor is usually able to work with models created with the old version of the metamodel, but without the ability to make user changes. For example, in MetaEdit+ [73], when an item is deleted from a metamodel, it continues to be visible and editable in older models, but new items of this type cannot be created and older items are marked as obsolete, and it is possible to get a list of obsolete model items.

In addition, support for language evolution is needed, not only for users but also for DSL authors. For example, the language metamodel should be stored in a version control system, and integration with such systems is desirable for the platform (although not mandatory, due to the availability of mature and user-friendly individual tools). It should be possible to compare different versions of metamodels.

It is also desirable to be able to analyze the use of the created language in "working" conditions [13]. In the implementation of the DSL, it may be possible to collect statistics on the use of language elements, statistics on user errors that occur, and the frequency of changes to properties and default settings. This will help the authors to identify unused or misused elements and the relevance of the proposed defaults and to make appropriate changes to the language description in order to improve its usability.

However, as previously mentioned, in existing DSL implementation tools, support for DSL evolution is either not implemented at all or is limited [70]. In visual DSL development environments, such support is implemented at the metamodel level and is not transferred to the syntax level, which may not be defined at all for this type of DSL [72]. On the other hand, in textual DSLs, grammar underlies everything, and as a consequence, when the DSL is changed, the grammar changes, which makes it impossible for the user to match the new DSL to the previous version, because they are both described in grammatical form and effort is required to extract the metamodel from the grammatical description [110]. It is much more effective to see an approach that combines the capabilities of both types of DSL implementation environments—a metamodel evolution toolkit similar to visual DSLs and further evolution of specific syntax by determining the correspondence between language commands and their equivalents at the metamodel level. This unified model-oriented approach to DSL development and evolution will allow real-time changes to the DSL without the need to completely re-create it, thereby realizing continuous evolution of the DSL.

This is also appropriate because the stages of the DSL lifecycle do not necessarily run sequentially. In most cases, the software development process is iterative, so most of the steps can be repeated over time to achieve the best quality of the developed software and its full compliance with the domain and user requirements.

The most important thing in this lifecycle is the fact that the design and development of the DSL is based on the results of the domain analysis. This means that in order to develop the DSL effectively, we need to have a formal tool that allows us to display the results of our domain analysis and which can then be applied to the DSL design.

Unfortunately, most of the existing approaches to DSL development adhere to a different idea, according to which the domain analysis stage may end with the capture of domain information in some structured form, which, however, is subsequently used in an informal form. Thus, for example, in the works [33, 54, 61], the process of DSL development begins with the stage of defining language components, that is, its syntactic component, while in fact it can be argued that all objects to be reflected in the structure of the DSL can and should be derived from the analysis of the subject domain. Otherwise, the duplication of the analysis already carried out occurs, which multiplies the time of the development of the DSL [116].

Furthermore, the absence of a formalized representation of the results of the domain analysis and the manual design of the DSL leads to a situation where the entire DSL lifecycle is repeated when changes need to be made to the structure of the DSL at all its levels. This leads to a situation where we cannot ensure consistency between the previous version of the language and its updated version, because formally they are different languages. However, from a semantic point of view, both languages are implemented for the same domain and thus are fully consistent on the level of semantics. However, in order to ensure this continuous evolution of DSL, it is necessary to have a formal representation of the semantics of the language, which is based on the results of the analysis of the target domain. Consequently, it is necessary to find a tool to formalize the representation of the target domain, which can then be used to formally describe the semantics of the DSL.

2.3 Features of the Development and Operation of Software Systems in Dynamic Contexts

As we are looking at the application of a DSL within software systems, it is necessary to compare the process of its development and operation (including modifications) with similar processes for these systems.

For the purposes of this chapter, we restrict ourselves to general-purpose software systems that are designed to automate a broad class of user tasks within a certain domain [81]—in our case, used to automate information processing within information systems, which are a set of information contained in databases and information technologies and technical means supporting its processing [80].

Leaving the implementation of databases used within information systems out of the scope of the study [57], it can be argued that the lifecycle of a software system corresponds to the lifecycle of a more general information system [20]. Therefore, in what follows, we consider the lifecycle of information systems as a whole.

Information systems are nowadays increasingly complex software environments. In the past, each individual program was assumed to execute one or more functions (as pointed out by M. Fernandez-Lopez in [35]). Information systems are now more service-oriented in the sense that they consist of a set of interconnected modules, each responsible for its own functionality (this approach is followed, in particular, by T. Cleenewerck in [24] and E. Evans in [33]).

As a consequence, each change to the information system as a whole can lead to the need to cascade changes to many of its individual parts and the links between them [24]. It is all the more important to ensure that each individual component of the information system can be modified independently. It is also important from the point of view that the individual components of an information system may be used by different categories of users responsible for different tasks.

It is for this reason that the information system lifecycle now includes the following stages in accordance with GOST R ISO/IEC 12207-2010 [46].

The Decision to Develop the System

At this stage, the customer's problem is analyzed, and a decision is made as to whether a complete information system or other software tool should be developed.

Requirements Analysis

This stage focuses on formulating the basic requirements for the future system, both on the end user side (user requirements) and on the customer-owner side (business requirements).

Designing the (Detailed) Architecture of the System

The result of this step is the construction of the top-level system architecture in the form of the technical, software, and manual parts. It must be ensured that all system requirements are allocated to these parts.

Implementation of the System (Including Design and Bundling)

At this stage, in accordance with the previously outlined architecture, the system is fully implemented: first in the form of individual components (design) and then in their integration into a single system (bundling).

System Testing

The main purpose of this stage is to compare the resulting system with the previously identified requirements and to rectify any defects identified.

Implementation of the System and Support and Maintenance of the System

This stage focuses on ensuring that the implemented system is operational, as well as on modifying it to meet new customer requirements as they arise.

This stage is the least studied, as it most often depends on the implementation language of the information system, the number of end users, the number of modules in the information system, etc. [36, 64].

Thus, the main stages of the lifecycle of information systems (and consequently of software systems) correspond to the lifecycle of a DSL. However, there is a contradiction in the maintenance of information systems and DSLs: in the case of information systems, support and maintenance are compulsory lifecycle stages, whereas in the case of DSLs, these stages are almost always absent and are not implemented in existing DSL development tools. Thus, in the case of DSLs used within information systems, there is a need to develop approaches and methods to organize the modification of the DSL in accordance with the changes made to the information system and, consequently, to the software system.

This becomes all the more important as the division of the software system used within an information system into visual and functional blocks makes it even more difficult to make changes to it in an automated way [24]. This is primarily due to the fact that individual end users have different experiences with information systems and have their own preferences and competencies. As a consequence, they can use the information system in different ways, thus resulting in the need to modify it to meet emerging new requirements. The result is a set of information systems that are identical in functionality but different in visual presentation [103].

In order to simplify this model of changing the information system to meet the requirements of users and to implement the transfer of these changes to the level of a DSL used within the information system, we consider it appropriate to consider the visual component of the information system in the form of OWL. This is efficient and reasonable from the point of view of the fact that the graphical interface of the information system has a limited functionality (directly related to the functionality of the system as a whole), just like the DSL, and in this sense, it can be considered as a special kind of DSL [61]. This is why incorporating elements of the evolution of DSLs into the evolution of information systems can be effective and provide greater flexibility for the latter with respect to the requirements of different categories of users [25].

2.4 Analysis of the Classical Approach to the Development of a DSL

On the basis of the above, we can formulate the main points of the classical methodology for developing a general-purpose software system DSL [33] and analyze them (Fig. 2.2).

We omit the decision-making and implementation phases because they are not directly related to DSL development in the sense that the decision-making only affects whether the DSL will in principle be developed or its more convenient software counterpart, while the implementation phase is related to the finished DSL

Fig. 2.2 The classic
approach to the development
of DSLs

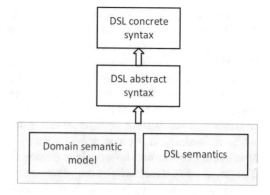

and does not depend on the form in which it is implemented. The most significant for us are the stages of analysis of the domain and the further design and implementation of the DSL on the basis of the analysis.

In the case of the classical DSL methodology (Fig. 2.2), there is a gap between the domain analysis stage and the direct design and implementation of the DSL. This gap is caused by the fact that the semantic model of the domain is used only informally in the process of domain analysis; the designers of the DSL only rely on it in the process of defining the semantics of the DSL. Consequently, the definition of DSL semantics is done manually, and later, when changes are made to the semantic model of the domain, adjustments to DSL semantics must also be done manually.

Thus, duplication of work is found, which also leads to the impossibility of automating the main stages of the DSL development in the case of the classical methodology and makes it impossible to organize the evolution of the DSL, since the modification of the DSL actually creates a new DSL [24].

Furthermore, since the syntax of the DSL (both abstract and concrete) is also formed manually on the basis of the semantics of the DSL, in case of changes in the semantic model of the domain, DSL developers have to make changes on the level of the DSL syntax as well. Such "divergent" modifications to the DSL when it needs to be adapted to changes in the semantic model of the domain make the process of organizing DSL evolution a time-consuming and complex process, making it virtually impossible to automate.

In addition, any change to the DSL can only be made by experts with appropriate programming skills, since end users cannot directly change the syntax of a language described in terms of a grammar not related to their domain. This results in a situation where the DSL becomes irrelevant over time and loses its primary purpose of being strictly relevant to the domain.

Some attempts have been made in the literature to address these limitations of the classical DSL methodology. For example, the works of Bell [10] provide examples of the implementation of a family of DSL dialects based on a single grammatical structure. However, this approach requires the implementation of a single and complete grammatical structure of the DSL without solving the problem of its further modification when the subject domain model changes.

Thus, there is a need to develop a different approach to the development of the DSL which would not only allow the results of each individual stage of the DSL lifecycle to be presented formally but would also allow them to be used in subsequent stages. To this end, a model-oriented approach is proposed that would allow each level of the DSL structure to be represented as a model, making it possible to make changes at different levels of the DSL independent of each other while maintaining coherence between them. In doing so, transitions between all levels of the DSL structure (models) are made through cross-model transformations. The proposed approach will be described in more detail in Sect. 2.1.

In this case, the results of the lifecycle stages are not only recorded as artifacts but are also used in the implementation of subsequent lifecycle stages. Such an organization of the design and development of a DSL allows not only the automation of the main stages of the DSL lifecycle but also its continuous evolution in the future. The main advantage of such a scheme is the consistency of new language dialects with previous ones at the metamodel (and semantics) level, which allows end users to customize and modify the DSL in real time without the need for manual changes at all levels of the DSL structure.

The classical approach to DSL development for modeling general-purpose human-machine interfaces of software systems thus has a number of shortcomings. In particular, the lifecycle of DSLs and software systems do not fully correspond to each other, since in the case of software systems, the support and maintenance phase with modification capability is mandatory, while in the case of DSLs, this lifecycle phase is optional and is not supported by most existing DSL development platforms.

In addition, there is a duplication of processes in the DSL development process using the classical approach: for example, a semantic model of the domain is formed at the stage of domain analysis, which is not subsequently used in a formal form when defining the semantics of the DSL manually. As a consequence, when changes are made to the semantic model of the domain, both the semantic model of the DSL and the DSL syntax must also be manually corrected.

These disadvantages of the classical approach make it impossible to automate the main stages of the DSL lifecycle and do not allow its evolution, as any change at all levels of the DSL structure is done manually and leads to the creation of a new DSL that is not consistent with the previous DSL. This disadvantage becomes critical in the case of general-purpose DSLs during their maintenance and modification to meet user requirements.

To address the shortcomings of the classical approach, a model-based representation of all levels of the DSL structure is proposed, with organization of the DSL development process through cross-model transformations between different models: the semantic domain model, the semantic DSL model, and the DSL metamodel.

A good tool for achieving these goals can be the use of conceptual models (namely, ontological models) of the domain. This is reasonable from the position of organizing the mentioned possibility of a seamless transition from the domain model to the DSL model, as well as the possibility of automated checking the consistency of the developed language with the semantic domain model. In addition, since the ontology allows us to describe not only the entities of the domain and the relationships between them but also the constraints of the domain, we get the possibility of transferring functional (behavioral) aspects from the semantic model of the domain for their subsequent implementation at the DSL level.

Chapter 3
Analysis of Existing Approaches to the Formalization of the DSL Structure

Abstract In this chapter, taking into account the critical aspects highlighted in the previous chapter, the main existing approaches to the formal definition of a DSL in general, from the semantic model to a specific syntax, will be analyzed. It is important to note that these methods will be considered in general terms, without reference to a particular type of DSL (graphical or textual) and to DSL development tools. This approach will allow to consider the structure of the DSL as a whole and to identify common components at different levels of the DSL structure in order to further integrate them and create a unified approach to creating a coherent DSL structure that allows its flexibility and evolution.

3.1 Approaches to the Development and Analysis of the Domain Semantic Model

The domain semantic model (DSM) is a flexible and compact way of defining domain data [13]. A DSM can represent some small fragments of knowledge about a domain (e.g., a small taxonomy with a few rules) as well as complex ontologies (derived by translating existing ontologies and adding rules and descriptors) [43]. For the purpose of this study, we use the notion of ontology in line with the work of Guizzardi [43, 44], who defines an ontology as "a representative artefact containing a conceptual representation of a domain in the form of a set of classes (concepts) and relations between them with a corresponding set of constraints". Depending on which version of the DSM structure is chosen, there will be one or another level of granularity of knowledge about the subject area. From a formal point of view, a DSM is a set of seven elements [48]:

$$DSM = (H_C, H_R, O, R, A, M, D) \tag{3.1}$$

where:

- H_C and H_R represent sets of classes and relations between them. The classes contain a set of attributes, and each attribute type is also a class. In both sets,

H_C and H_R are defined partial orders to represent concepts and relationship taxonomies, respectively.

- O and R are sets of class objects and relations between them, also called objects and tuples, respectively.
- A is a set of axioms described by special rules expressing the constraints of the subject area.
- M is a set of inference modules, which are logical programs consisting of a set of (disjunctive) rules that allow reasoning about the knowledge presented and stored, as well as inferring new, not previously explicitly declared, knowledge.
- D is a set of descriptors (i.e., inference rules in a two-dimensional object-oriented attribute grammar) that allows the recognition of class instances (concepts) contained in O, as well as their annotations.

It is also important to note that DSM tends to have a dynamic structure. Any domain exhibits a tendency to change over time (in other words, an evolutionary tendency). In line with the evolution of the domain, the corresponding DSM also evolves [102]. As a result, any DSL based on the corresponding DSM must be modified to align the structure of the DSL with changes in the target domain. Consequently, the structure of the DSL metamodel should be as close as possible to that of the DSM in order to ensure consistency between the DSL and the target domain. Thus, it is prudent to select a common meta-metamodel to be used both for defining the DSL metamodel and for the DSM [103]. We believe that a widely used object-oriented metamodel, especially ontologies, may be suitable for this purpose. In order to justify this assumption, it is necessary to consider the definition of DSM as a special kind of object-oriented model and to define it using ontological approach.

3.2   Definition and Classification of Ontologies

Before talking about the mechanisms of establishing a correspondence between the domain model and the DSL, it is necessary to define the concept of ontology.

Among specialists dealing with the problems of computational linguistics, the definition of ontology given by Hubert is considered the most established (classical) definition: "ontology is a specification of conceptualization" [42]. A number of extended definitions are also known, among which one will be used in what follows.

Ontology is a representational artifact, comprising a taxonomy as proper part, whose representations are intended to designate some combination of universals, defined classes, and certain relations between them [43].

According to this definition, the following considerations can be deduced: (1) the ontology is a representational artifact = def. the scheme of certain domain; (2) the ontology contains concepts of certain domain and its properties and relations between them; and (3) a proper part of relations are taxonomy-type relations.

Based on these considerations, the ontology can be represented as a triple (O, R, F), where $O = U \bigcup C$ is a set of objects, $U = \{u_1, u_2, \ldots, u_N\}$, $N \in \mathbb{N}$ (where u_i, $i = 1, N$ is a concept (universal) of a certain area and can be represented as a set of its attributes $u_i = \{attr_1, attr_2, \ldots, attr_M\}$, $M \in \mathbb{N}$, , $i = 1, N$), C (class) is a set of c_i, $i = 1, K$, $K \in \mathbb{N}$, where c_i is an exemplar of some u_j, R is a set of relations between elements of O, and F is an interpretation function assigning values to the non-logical constants of the language [44].

From this point of view, the ontology can be naturally perceived as a graph (O, R), with a set of functions of constraints F.

On the other hand, the ontology is some kind of representation, created by the designer [43]. From this point of view, development of the ontology has always some certain goal, which affects the whole design process and its final result, the ontology itself.

Since ontologies were the answer of science to the needs of their time, their appearance occurred simultaneously in several areas of knowledge. Accordingly, in each of them, resources of the ontological type were formed according to their own rules specific to the field of knowledge. The same point of view is shared by the authors of [82], who believe that in the design of ontologies, it is conditionally possible to distinguish two directions, which until some time developed separately.

The first is related to the representation of ontology as a formal system based on mathematically exact axioms (i.e., these are resources of an ontological type created in various areas of mathematics).

The second direction developed within the framework of computational linguistics and cognitive science. Here, ontology was understood as a system of abstract concepts that exist only in the human mind, which can be expressed in a natural language (or by means of some other system of symbols). In this case, no assumptions are usually made about the accuracy or consistency of such a system.

Thus, there are two alternative approaches to the creation and study of ontologies. The first (formal) is based on logic (first-order predicates, descriptive, modal, etc.). The second (linguistic) is based on the study of natural language (in particular, semantics) and the construction of ontologies on large text arrays, the so-called corpora.

There are various types of classification of ontologies. From our point of view, it will be most useful to single out two types of classification of ontologies: semantic and pragmatic ones. We give a brief description of each classification.

Semantic classification includes the following ontology types:

- *According to the level of expressiveness*:

  - *Heavyweight ontologies.* Heavyweight ontologies are strongly axiomatized; this level of axiomatization allows explicit ontological binding. The goal of axiomatization is to avoid terminological and conceptual ambiguity due to misinterpretation. Every heavyweight ontology can have a lightweight version. Many ontologies of subject areas (domain) are heavy, because they should support processes for building complex inferences. As in the definition of any size, the boundary between heavyweight and lightly weighted ontologies is blurred.

– *Lightweight ontologies*. These are simple taxonomic structures of primitives or compositions of terms with corresponding definitions. They are weakly axiomatized, since the meaning of a term used within a community is usually more or less known to all members of the community. Accordingly, links between terms that are considered relevant can be represented in the ontology to a limited extent.

• **By the degree of formality**: this classification is similar to the classification by the level of expressiveness of the language ontology description (see the previous paragraph), but is not equivalent to it.

– *Informal*. These ontologies are described in a document in any natural language (English, German, etc.). Despite the absence of formal assignment rules, such ontologies can also be richly filled, consistent, and precise.

– *More formalized*. Taxonomy can be of two types—based on terms or based on concepts. Such ontologies, although formalized, are very weakly structured, for example, structured by links "narrower than" or "subclass" based on terms. In this case, in the hierarchy of the thematic section, more general terms are higher, and as you go down the hierarchy, the terms become more and more specific: concept-based. The hierarchy consists of classes and their subclasses, which display their distinctive and necessary properties.

– *Heavily formalized*. Ontologies for solving engineering equations. They define the formal semantics of terms (such as quantity and unit of measurement) in precise and consistent expressions allowed by the language.

• **By the level of detail of the presentation**: some quantifiable metrics can be applied to the calculation of the level of detail of the presentation, for example, the average depth of the structure of subclasses/subattributes (subproperties), average grouping/bushiness (bushiness), the number of axioms, and others.

– *Low*. An ontology can be built on the basis of terms and several types of relationships, for example, a very formal ontology, described in terms of common logic (Common Logic), but containing only three classes and two properties.

– *High*. An ontology can contain much more detail, including the rules by which terms can be related, for example, very detailed description of biological classes and their distinctive features in natural language or a very formal ontology, described in one of the languages KIF, CL, and OWL+SWRL, which contain thousands of classes, properties, rules, and millions of instances/individuals.

From the pragmatic point of view, the following classification of ontology kinds can be identified [44]:

• **According to the degree of dependence on a specific task or application domain of the upper level**: such ontologies describe the most general concepts (space,

time, matter, object, event, action, etc.) that are independent of a specific problem
or domain.

- *Domain-oriented*. Many communities are now developing standard ontologies
  that can be used by domain experts to share and annotate information in
  their field. For example, in the field of medicine, large standard, structured
  vocabularies have been created, such as SNOMED and the Semantic Web
  of the Unified Medical Language System, or extensive general-purpose
  ontologies.
- *Task-oriented*. It is an ontology used by a specific application program and
  contains terms that are used in the development of software that performs a
  specific task. It reflects the specifics of the application, but may also contain
  some general terms (e.g., in the graphical editor, there will be specific terms,
  palette, fill type, overlay layers, etc., and general terms, save and load the file).
- *Applied (application) ontologies* describe concepts that depend on both the
  task ontology and the domain ontology. An example is the ontology for cars,
  building materials, and computer technology.

- **By the language of ontological knowledge representation**:

  - *RDF*. The language was developed as part of the Semantic Web project.
    The main purpose of the language is to describe the metadata of documents
    posted on the Internet. RDF uses the basic data representation model "object-
    attribute-value" and is able to play the role of a universal language for
    describing the semantics of resources and relationships between them.
  - *DAML+OIL* is a semantic markup language for Web resources that extends the
    RDF and RDF Schema standards with more complete modeling primitives.
    The latest version of DAML+OIL includes a set of additional constructs for
    creating ontologies and marking up information in a machine-readable form.
  - *OWL (Web Ontology Language)* is the next-generation ontology represen-
    tation language after DAML+OIL. It has a richer feature set than XML,
    RDF, RDF Schema, and DAML+OIL. The project involves the creation of
    a powerful semantic analysis mechanism. It is planned that it will eliminate
    the limitations of the DAML+OIL designs. An OWL ontology is a sequence
    of axioms, facts, and references to other ontologies.
  - *KIF (Knowledge Interchange Format, or knowledge exchange format)* based
    on S-expressions syntax for logic. KIF is a special language designed for the
    exchange of knowledge between different computer systems. It was developed
    to describe a general format for representing knowledge, independent of
    specific systems.
  - *CycL* is a hybrid language that combines the properties of frames and predicate
    logic. The syntax of CycL is similar to that of Lisp. CycL distinguishes
    between entities such as instances, classes, predicates, and functions. The
    CycL dictionary consists of terms. The set of terms can be divided into
    constants, nonatomic terms, and variables. Terms are used in the construction

of meaningful expressions of CycL, from which judgments are formed. The knowledge base consists of judgments.

– *OCML (Operational Conceptual Modeling Language)* supports the construction of several types of knowledge representation constructs. It allows you to specify and operationalize functions, relationships, classes, instances, and rules. It also includes mechanisms for describing ontologies and methods for solving problems—the main technologies developed in the field of knowledge representation. About a dozen projects at KMI (Knowledge Media Institute) currently use OCML to develop models in areas such as knowledge management, ontology development, e-commerce, and knowledge processing systems.

– *Loom/PowerLoom* is a knowledge representation language developed by researchers from the Artificial Intelligence Research Group at the University of Southern California's Information Sciences Institute. The goal of the Loom project is to develop and implement advanced tools for knowledge representation and reasoning in the field of artificial intelligence. Loom and PowerLoom are distributed under open-source licenses, but are the intellectual property of the University of Southern California and are not in the public domain. Loom is both a language and a framework for building intelligent applications. The center of the language is the knowledge representation system, which is used to build deductive conclusions based on declarative knowledge. Declarative knowledge consists of definitions, rules, facts, and default rules. The deductive engine uses direct inference chains, semantic unification, and object-oriented technologies for maintaining reliability.

– *Ontolingua* provides a distributed environment for collaborative viewing, creating, editing, modifying, and using ontologies. The server supports over 150 active users. Ontolingua consists of a KIF parser, tools for ontology analysis, and a set of translators for converting Ontolingua source data into a form acceptable for implementation in knowledge representation systems.

– *F-Logic* is an ontological language that is based on first-order logics, but classes and properties are represented as terms, not as predicates. The language was created to implement the interaction between ontologies built on the basis of predicates and ontologies built on the basis of F-Logic. The creators have defined intuitive translators for transforming knowledge from predicate ontologies into F-Logic ontologies and have shown that such a translation preserves logical connections (preserves entailment) for a large number of ontological languages, including many OWL DLs. Also, the language can be used for metamodeling extensions of description logics (v-semantics).

• **By the target domain**: ontology reflects general knowledge about the target domain, such as the hierarchy of classes of concepts and semantic relations on these classes. For each subject area, ontologies are created by experts in their field who formalize knowledge, definitions, and rules for obtaining new knowledge.

To create and maintain ontologies, there are both specifications and tools (i.e., mentioned above).

- **_According to the purpose of creating_**:

  - *Application ontology.* They are used during the execution of a specific application that performs ontological application of restrictions on axiomatization for a terminological service, i.e., are used in the work of the reasoning building block. The typical tradeoff between expressiveness and decidability requires a limited representation of the formalisms. In applications built on the principles of descriptive logics (DL), this will be the same as TBox. Application ontologies can also describe concrete worlds (semantic descriptions, knowledge bases, metadata, semantic metadata, or just instances). In applications based on descriptive logics, this will be the same as ABox.
  - *Reference ontologies.* Used during application development, for mutual understanding and interpretation between agents belonging to different communities, to establish consensus between communities that need to introduce a new term, or simply to explain the meaning of a term to a new member of the community. Although parts of a reference ontology can also be formalized as TBox, however, descriptive logics are usually not expressive enough to be used as references.

- **_By filling (content)_**: this classification is very similar to the classification by the purpose of creation, but the emphasis is on the real content of the ontology and not on the abstract goal pursued by the authors.

Additionally, other classifications can be introduced. For example, ontologies can also be divided into monolingual and multilingual. There are already a number of ontologies focused on the representation of knowledge in several languages, for example, EuroWordNet, MikroKosmos, and some others. The complexity of creating such ontologies usually lies in the fact that there may be differences in the conceptual systems of different languages.

Also, all ontologies can be divided into deep and surface. Surface ontologies are built on surface semantics, and they define concepts through the meanings of words. However, here the problem arises, how many meanings to allocate for each word. Deep ontologies use deep semantics.

Sometimes, lexical (linguistic) ontologies are included in the classification as a separate type. A distinctive feature of such ontologies is the fixation in one resource of (lexicalized) concepts (words) together with their linguistic properties. Such ontologies are closely interconnected with the semantics of grammatical elements (words, noun phrases, etc.). The main source of concepts in ontologies of this type are the meanings of linguistic units. They are also distinguished by a peculiar set of relations, usually characteristic of linguistic elements: synonymy, hyponymy, meronymy, and a number of others. Linguistic ontologies include WordNet, MikroKosmos, Sensus, RuThes, and others. The range of tasks solved by such ontologies is closely related to natural language processing.

In the current research, we pay attention only to the application ontologies, especially in the domain of railway processes—the railway resource allocation procedure. But as the domain ontology contains only the necessary concepts of a target domain, applied ontology operates with a subset of these concepts necessary to achieve a certain goal. That allows us to consider the application ontology as the reduced domain ontology.

After we have decided on the type of ontology under consideration, it is also necessary to mention the principles of its construction. There are the following principles of ontology construction: (1) Cyc approach; (2) method of Uskold and King; (3) Grüninger and Fox methodology; and (4) METHONTOLOGY methodology.

The Cyc approach was formed during the implementation of a project to create a super-large knowledge base. Within its framework, the first knowledge engineering tools were developed, the knowledge representation language CycL, the base technologies of ontology, which served as the calculus of predicates of higher orders and the language of systems. The idea of structuring the knowledge base in the form of microtheories, including knowledge from different domains presented from different points of view, was also proposed.

Uskold and King's method was proposed based on the results of the development of one of the most famous ontologies of business process modeling—the enterprise ontology; a methodology for designing ontologies was developed, in which they formulated the following steps: (1) defining the goal, (2) ontology development (ontology fixation, ontology coding, integration), (3) evaluation of the created ontology, and (4) documentation. Defining the goal is necessary for a clear understanding of why the ontology was created and for what purposes it will be used. It will also be used to determine the range of users of the ontology. Building an ontology includes (1) determination of key concepts and links in the required domain (scoping); (2) development of precise, consistent textual definitions for these concepts and relationships; (3) definition of terms related to such concepts and relationships; and (4) coordination of all of the above. By coding is meant the exact representation of the details fixed in the previous stage in some formal language. This includes fixing a particular meta-ontology, choosing a representation language, and creating a description of the ontology in that language. At the stages of fixation and coding, the question often arises whether it is possible to somehow use existing ontologies. In general, this is a very difficult problem, although, for example, the Ontolingua project has made significant progress in this direction. The development of guidance and tools in this area would be one of the most significant breakthroughs in the development of an integrated methodology. Evaluation means to provide a technical opinion on an ontology and its associated software environment and documentation, regarding criteria. Criteria can be specification requirements, questions of competence, and/or real world. Documentation may be desirable to define recommendations for documenting ontologies, possibly different, depending on the type and purpose of the ontology.

The Grüninger and Fox methodology is based on the experience of developing a certain specific ontology, with domain-oriented business process modeling, and involves the creation of an ontology as a logical knowledge model; it consists of the following stages: (1) fixing the motivational scenario, (2) formulating informal questions for testing competence, (3) ontology terminology specifications in a formal language (obtained informal ontology, specification of formal terminology), (4) formulation of questions for assessing competence using terms, 5) axiom specifications for ontology terms in a formal language, and 6) setting the conditions for the completeness of the ontology.

A distinctive feature of the METHONTOLOGY methodology is its formation on the basis of the analysis and rethinking of the main activities inherent in the processes of software development and knowledge engineering. The METHON-TOLOGY methodology integrates the experience of designing complex objects from two areas of knowledge. It includes the identification of the ontology development process and lifecycle based on the evolution of prototypes and individual techniques for performing any activity.

Thus, currently, there is no description of a unified and correct methodology for compiling an ontology, but axioms for their creation have been formulated.

Axiom 1: There is no right way to model a domain because there are always good alternatives. The optimal solution depends on the intended outcome.

Axiom 2: The development and description of ontologies is always of a constant iterative nature.

Axiom 3: Concepts in an ontology are always directly related to physical or logical objects, as well as relationships in a particular domain. Thus, modeling is primarily influenced by the purpose of creating an ontology, as well as its detailing.

In addition, the principles of ontology construction described above, according to T. Gruber [44]:

- *Clarity*, i.e., the ontology effectively conveys the meaning of the introduced terms, which must be objective or given by logical axioms.
- *Consistency*, i.e., all definitions are logically consistent verbal, and the statements in the ontology do not contradict the axioms.
- *Extensibility*, i.e., the ontology must ensure the use of dictionaries of terms that allow the possibility of expansion.
- *Minimum influence of coding*, i.e., the ontology is specified on presentation level, not character encoding.
- *Minimum of ontological obligations*, i.e., the ontology contains only the most essential assumptions about the modeled world in order to leave the freedom of expansion.

Thus, ontologies are based on "weak" theories, since the main purpose of their use is a description of the domain, in contrast to knowledge bases that contain inference rules and information about person experience.

In addition to these principles can be formalized the following five principles:

- *The principle of completeness.* The top-level categories must exhaustively repre-sent matter; outside these categories, there should be no manifestations of beings.
- *The principle of natural science and problem orientation.* All categories and concepts of ontology should be expressed by concepts that have been established in the natural and mathematical sciences in the study of the material world and are generally accepted. At the same time, a part of the ontology should be represented by concepts that are widely used in interdisciplinary texts (with neutral, generally accessible vocabulary), and the second part of the ontology is structured for a specific area of knowledge (KbA). The first part has a permanent status, while the problem-oriented ontology is formed by a specialist and is of a variable nature.
- *The principle of interconnectedness of levels.* Top-level ontology categories are revealed by sets of middle-level concepts. In turn, the concepts of the lower level should serve as determinants for the terms of the KbA dictionary. The connection between the middle and lower levels is organized with the help of named relations of the form "to be a part", "to belong to a set", "to coincide with", and "to be in semantic relationship with".
- *The principle of associativity.* The concepts of the lower-level ontology should serve as a field for indexing the terms of the KbA. In this case, semantic relations of the form are used: "to be in an associative connection with".
- *The principle of reflection of antagonisms.* Concepts that reflect properties or concepts that have their opposite or complementarity on an equal footing are included in the ontology in pairs or triplets of polar designations.

Therefore, for high-quality problem processing, it is necessary to have a detailed description of the problem area with many logical connections that show the relationship between the terms of the area. The use of ontologies makes it possible to represent a natural language text in such a way that it becomes suitable for automatic processing.

Additionally, ontologies can be used as an intermediary between the user and the information system, which makes it possible to formalize the terms used between all users of the project.

Also, the problems of ontological analysis have found wide application. Within the framework of these tasks, with the help of ontological research, valuable information about the functioning of complex systems is accumulated. Such an analysis usually begins with the compilation of a glossary of terms, which is used in the discussion and study of the characteristics of objects and processes that make up the system under consideration, as well as the creation of a system of precise definitions of these terms. In addition, the main logical relationships between the relevant terms and concepts are documented. The result of this analysis is a dictionary of terms, their exact definitions, and relationships between them. The information collected is used in the process of reorganizing existing or building new systems that is the main focus of DSL application in our work.

3.3 Languages and Visualization Tools for Ontologies as DSM

Visualization of ontologies is not an easy task, since in addition to the hierarchy, ontologies contain associative links between classes, which must also be visualized [38]. Moreover, the sizes of ontologies are steadily growing, and even now, there are ontologies consisting of several thousand classes. Each class, as a rule, includes instances, the number of which can also reach several thousand. It is far from always reasonable and efficient to show classes and instances in the same image. And finally, there are ontologies in which the same class can have several parents, which significantly complicates the process of effectively visualizing the taxonomy.

As part of this work, it was decided to focus on visualizing only classes (and the relationships between them). If necessary, the user can view the list of instances present in the ontology using alternative methods.

One of the most common and generally accepted ways of visualizing information is visualization using graph models [26, 44], including using a layer-by-level algorithm [26], a radial algorithm [38], etc. These visualization algorithms are widely used in many information visualization tools. Despite this, they all have one significant drawback: as a result of their work, a static image is obtained, and this becomes a problem even for small ontologies. The static nature of the image limits the user's actions and makes it impossible to study in detail the individual parts of the ontology. Because of this, there is a need for interactive navigation and visualization methods that would allow you to control the visualization result depending on the needs of the user.

In this regard, interactive visualization gives the user the opportunity to study ontologies in a simpler and more understandable way [48]. For example, scalable rendering [49] is used in many visualization systems and allows the user to change the scale of an image area of interest to him. In this case, two types of scaling are distinguished—geometric and semantic. Geometric scaling simply increases (or reduces) the size of visualization elements, while semantic scaling adds (or removes) new elements to the image that were not visible before, based on some heuristic. Also, scalable rendering allows users to change the position of the image relative to the viewport.

Incremental visualization systems [50], instead of drawing large graphs as a whole, depict them as small and understandable subgraphs. Such systems draw only the visible parts of a large image and allow the user to move around the graph, adding new elements as they go. Since such systems do not need to draw the entire graph, they often have faster user response times and lower computational complexity than other systems.

Visualization systems based on the "focus + context" technique [54] create an image in which the information of interest to the user (focus) is shown in full detail and for the rest of the information (context), only a superficial overview is given. The user can interact with such systems by changing the focus, thereby changing the image itself. "Focus + context" group methods use various space distortion algorithms and are usually divided into two categories: (1) distortion occurs after the graph is imaged, and (2) distortion is built into the visualization algorithm itself.

Finally, there are hybrid models based on common modeling languages (conceptual metamodels) and their dialects that combine the advantages of all the methods mentioned above. Examples of such languages are ER [54] and UML [26] and its variant OntoUML [44].

One of the best known conceptual metamodels is entity relationship (ER). However, the popularity of ER is also its main weakness: the metamodel is simple, despite the fact that this assists conceptual modelers. However, the metamodel is not highly expressive.

UML is also a well-known language for building conceptual models, but it has the same problem of expressiveness [43]. The concepts from a universe of discourse are abstract entities that often exist only in the minds of users. To capture these concepts, they must be represented through concrete artifacts. This means a language must represent them in a concise, complete, and unambiguous manner. A language that has flaws of expressiveness may compromise understanding of requirements artifacts in later phases.

Considering these issues, Guizzardi proposed OntoUML [44], which is a language used to represent ontology-based conceptual models. Because the language is ontology-based, the conceptual models constructed in OntoUML are assumed to be more expressive and to represent the real world of the domain more faithfully than do other languages of conceptual representation. The constructs proposed in OntoUML prevent the overload and redundancy found in other languages such as UML.

In this study, only the main constructs that comprise the object type category are presented. In this category, constructs are more closely related to the conceptual modeling of a domain [43].

The object type constructs may be sortal and non-sortal. Sortals provide identity and individuation principles to their instances, whereas non-sortals do not supply any clear identification principles. Sortal constructs are classified as rigid and anti-rigid sortals. A sortal is said to be rigid if it is necessarily applied to all its instances in all possible worlds. A sortal is said to be anti-rigid if it is not necessarily applied to all its instances. Rigid sortals include kind and subkind categories. A kind is a rigid sortal and thus has intrinsic material properties that provide clear identity and individuation principles. It determines existentially independent classes of things or beings and is said to be functional complexes. A subkind is also a rigid type that provides an identity principle and has some restrictions established and related to the kind construct. Every object in a conceptual model must be an instance of only one kind.

Two sub-categories of anti-rigid sortals exist: phases and roles. In both cases, instances may change their types without affecting their identities. During the phase construct, changes may occur as a result of changes to intrinsic properties. By contrast, in the role construct, changes occur because of relational properties.

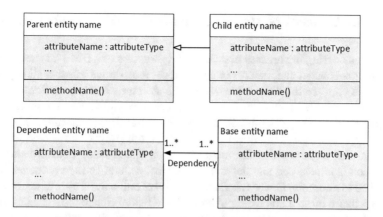

Fig. 3.1 Main elements of UML diagram for the ontology visualization

In what follows, we use UML class diagrams to display ontologies (see Fig. 3.1). Domain object types are represented by UML classes with the "type" stereotype. The type/subtype relationship is represented by the UML generalization relationship. Attributes whose types are built-in data types appear in the UML as class attributes, and attributes whose types are abstract data types appear as associations in the UML. Type attributes are represented by a text string of the form *attributeName : attributeType*, where *attributeType* is a programmatic specification of the attribute type. In the section under attributes, we can also designate a set of methods that can be applied to the corresponding entity.

Associations represent a semantic relationship between type instances. In our case, instead of a bidirectional association, we use a unidirectional relationship of the "dependency" type, which determines the (im)possibility of the existence of one object without another (Fig. 3.1, bottom). We also will use such a relation as inheritance (Fig. 3.1, top), which has an immediate correspondence to inheritance in object-oriented design. In both cases, the corresponding relation is visualized using corresponding arrow-line type. At each end of the line, there is optional notation. For example, the multiplicity of instances of that entity (the range of number of objects that participate in the association from the perspective of the other end) can be specified. We can also specify the name for the relation in order to make it more understandable for users.

Also, it's important to note that sometimes the diagram only shows the required elements, depending on the user's required perspective. For example, we can display only the names of entities and the relationships between them, hiding the sets of attributes and methods.

3.4   The Concept of Model-to-Model (M2M) Transformations

Before considering the process of defining the structure of a DSL, it is necessary to consider the concept and features of cross-model transformations that allow for full transitions between the different levels of DSL structure, from semantics to specific syntax. Cross-model transformation is the process by which a source model M_0 is transformed into a target model M_1 by applying a transformation rule R [1].

The structure and definition of cross-model transformations are inextricably linked to the way in which the model itself on which these transformations are performed is understood and defined. In its most general form, any model can be described as a combination of (E, R) of some set of entities and a set of relationships between them. From a graphical point of view, a model can be visualized by means of graphs whose structure is also based on entities and the relationships between them [49]. The structure of a graph is a combination of (V, R) of some set of vertices (visualizing entities) and links (arcs) between them.

By interpreting any vertex as the graphical equivalent of an entity and the arcs of a graph as the equivalents of relations between entities, we can say that any model can be described in a graph-oriented way. As a consequence, transformations between models can also be described by means of graph transformation rules.

Currently, model transformation methodologies have been developed extensively. However, all existing approaches can be divided into two groups:

- **Relational approaches** [1]: in these approaches, the transformation is usually defined in terms of the relationship between the objects (and the relationships between them) of the source and target modeling languages. Such a specification is usually based on a metamodel with OCL constraints.
- **Operational approaches** [2]: these methods describe the process of transforming a model from a source modeling language to a target language through (a) graph (model) transformations, (b) triple graph grammars, or (c) term rewriting rules.

According to these ideas, the cross-model transformation process can be described as follows (Fig. 3.2):

1. **Specification of modeling languages**. As a prerequisite, each modeling language (both A and B) must be precisely defined using metamodeling and graph (model) transformation techniques. In some studies (in particular [2, 14]), it has been demonstrated that many languages in MDA (Model Driven Architecture) implementations can have semantics defined in a visual way (which is closely related, for instance, to UML modeling techniques) [13].
2. **Specification of cross-model transformations**. Model transformation $A2B$ should also be defined by a set of (non-conflicting) graph (model) transformation rules. The practical feasibility of such a solution has been demonstrated in many articles, e.g., [14, 47, 49].
3. **Automated model generation**. For any given (but arbitrary) instance of a correctly generated source language model A, the corresponding target model

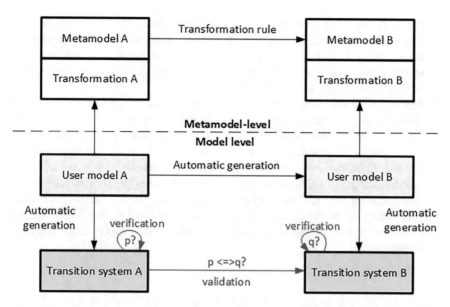

Fig. 3.2 Schematic diagram of the cross-model DSL transformation process

is derived using automatically generated conversion programs (e.g., generated by VIATRA [109] as a support tool).

4. **Transition system generation.** A system of behaviorally equivalent transitions is generated automatically for both the source and target models, based on validated coding.

5. **Select the semantic correctness property.** One semantic property (condition) is selected p (at a time) in the source language A, which is structurally expressed as a graphical template made up of elements of the original metamodel (and possibly some temporal logic operators) [39]. It is important to note that formalizing these criteria for a particular model transformation is a difficult task: although in many cases it is possible to reduce the issue to a reachability problem, even then finding suitable temporal logic formulas is non-trivial [30].

6. **Validation of the original model.** The transition system A is checked automatically (using existing model checking tools such as SPIN [93] or SAL (Symbolic Analysis Laboratory tools) [76]) to confirm the property (condition) p. This process of model validation must be successful; otherwise, there are inconsistencies in the source model itself (verification problem), or/and informal requirements are not adequately reflected by the property (condition) p (a validation problem has arisen), or the formal semantics of the source language is inappropriate because a counterexample has been found that must match the given informal expectations (another validation problem).

7. **Conversion and confirmation of the property.** At this point, the property (condition) p is converted to the property (condition) q in the target language (either manually or with the same conversion program). Because a potentially

erroneous model conversion may incorrectly convert a property (condition) p to a property (condition) q, subject matter experts must confirm that the property (condition) q is in fact the target equivalent of the property (condition) p or an amplified version of it. Unfortunately, this verification step usually requires human expertise and cannot be fully automated.

8. **Validation of the target model**. Finally, the transient system B is checked against a property (condition) q on the target model. If the test is successful, we conclude that the model transformation is correct with respect to a pair of (p, q) properties (conditions) for particular pairs of source and target models (A and B, respectively) whose semantics is determined by a set of graph transformation rules. Otherwise, the property (condition) p is not retained during model conversion, and debugging can be initiated based on the error trace obtained by the model checker. As in the cases described earlier, this debugging phase can correct problems in the model conversion or in the target language specification.

3.5   Defining Model Transformations Through Graphs and Invariants

Since the modeling language may represent an example of a domain-specific language (DSL), we assume to use a graph-oriented approach to the organization of model transformations, like described in [39]. Such approach is reasonable, since any model can be generalized as a set of interconnected entities in object-oriented manner with subsequent application of graph transformations for its development and evolution.

Graph transformation (see [93] for theoretical foundations) provides a rule-based manipulation of graphs, which is conceptually similar to the well-known Chomsky grammar rules but using graph patterns instead of textual ones. From the formal point of view, any graph transformation rule is represented be a triple $Rule = (L, \neg, R)$, where L is the left-hand side graph, R is the right-hand side graph, and $\neg$ is (an optional) negative application condition.

In these conditions, the application of a rule to a model (graph) M results in replacing the pattern defined by L with the pattern of the R. From an algorithmic point of view, this means that we find a *match* of the L pattern in model M; check the negative application condition $\neg$; remove a part of model M, mapped to the pattern L; and finally add new elements to the intermediate model IM, which exists in the R but cannot be mapped to the L yielding the derived model M.

Such mechanism is very close to the mechanism of finding inductive invariants, which describe the connection between components of two (or more) sets of objects and are denoted with inv_τ. For this type of invariants, two types of specifications are defined, *next* and *inv*:

$$next_\tau.(p, q).F \triangleq [p \implies \mathcal{W}.F.q] \,\hat{}\, inv_\tau.p.F \triangleq next_\tau.(p, p).F \wedge [\mathcal{J}.F \implies p]$$

Informally, $next_\tau.(p,q)$ means that whenever a transition is fired from a state that satisfies p, the resulting state satisfies q. Similarly, $inv_\tau.p$ specifies that p is true in any initial state and is preserved by every atomic transition. Therefore, by induction, p is true in every state. It should be noted that, since $[W.F.q \implies q]$ because of possible stuttering, $next_\tau.(p,q).F \implies [p \implies q]$.

According to the above definition, inductive invariant means that there is a strong correspondence between elements of two sets of objects, which are connected during some relation (transformation). Such definition is very close to the relational approach for model transformation definition, when relationship between objects (and links) of the source and target language are declared. That results in the idea that inductive invariant can be an effective mechanism for the definition of such model transformations and for the validation of the possibility of obtaining one model by transforming another.

In this case, graph transformation rules serve as elementary operations, while the entire operational semantics of a language or a model transformation is defined by a model transformation system, where the allowed transformation sequences are constrained by a control flow graph (CFG) applying a transformation rule in a specific rule application mode at each node. From this point of view, the transition system consists of the operational invariants and can be associated with a subset $O.F$ of $(\Sigma, F)^w$ of (in)finite sequences of states defined as follows.

An infinite computation $\sigma = \langle \sigma_0, \sigma_1, \ldots, \sigma_n, \ldots \rangle$ belongs to the set $O.F$ if and only if

$$\begin{cases} \mathcal{J}.F.\sigma_0 \\ \forall i \in \mathbb{N} : \mathcal{W}.F.\{\sigma_{i+1}\}.\sigma_i \end{cases}$$

where $\{\sigma_{i+1}\}$ is the state predicate that evaluates to *true* for the state σ_{i+1} and to *false* for any other state.

Informally, O consists of those sequences of states that begin with an initial state that satisfies J ($\neg$ negative application condition in our case) and in which each state has a successor in accordance with the transition W (*Rule* transformation rule in our case). The set O is nonempty because J is satisfiable and W includes stuttering steps.

Once the computations of a transition system are built, *next* and *inv* specifications are defined as expected:

$$next_\mathcal{O}.(p,q).F \triangleq \forall \sigma \in \mathcal{O}.F : \forall i \in \mathbb{N} : p, \sigma_i \implies q, \sigma_{i+1}$$

$$inv_\mathcal{O}.p.F \triangleq \forall \sigma \in \mathcal{O}.F : \forall i \in \mathbb{N} : p, \sigma_i$$

Informally, $next_O.(p,q)$ means that, in any computation of the system, any state that satisfies p is immediately followed by a state that satisfies q. Although computations include stuttering steps, $next_O.(p,q)$ does *not* imply that $[p \Rightarrow q]$. In the same way, $inv_O.p$ means that any state of any computation of a system satisfies

p. Naturally, $next_O$ and inv_O are related in a way similar to the relationship between $next_\tau$ and inv_τ, namely, $inv_O.p.F \equiv next_O.(p, q).F \wedge [J.F \implies p]$.

According to these principles, we can conclude that validation of the model transformation correctness can be fully described through invariant mechanisms. Such definition can allow us to automate the process of formal validation of the model transformation, reducing it to verifying the presence of invariants of both types among defined model (graph) transformations.

3.6 Model-Based Methods for Defining DSLs

This section discusses the main aspects of existing approaches to model-based definition of the structure of a DSL. Consideration of these methods will allow us to further define formal models of the evolution of a DSL at all levels of structure, from semantics to concrete syntax, thereby removing the constraints on the implementation of DSL evolution under the existing approaches discussed in the previous sections.

3.6.1 Three-Tiered Structure of the DSL

Like any language, a DSL, in its general form, contains a semantic and a syntactic component. The semantic component determines the semantic load of language syntax constructions, which, in turn, is divided into abstract syntax (defining the metamodel of the DSL) and concrete syntax (defining the functional features of the DSL) [34].

In order to introduce the concept of DSL evolution, it is necessary to first define the relationship between the different levels of the DSL structure (Fig. 3.3; note that * denotes the upper bound of cardinality in the association specification). This is important from the point of view that the evolution of the DSL implies changes in its structure, and thus, we need to understand how these or those changes will affect the structure of the DSL as a whole.

From the diagram provided (Fig. 3.3), it can be seen that the whole DSL structure is described by means of a metamodel, from which specific DSL models are created and used by end users [24].

In this case (Fig. 3.3), the abstract syntax of the DSL is defined in terms of a model that includes the set of objects used in the DSL. This model is described in terms of a metamodel (e.g., KM3 [49], Ecore [63], etc.). The transition from the abstract syntax model of the DSL to the levels of semantics and concrete syntax is made by defining mappings (cross-model transformations) (Fig. 3.4) that form the basis of a transducer (taking objects of the source model as input and generating target models as output). The transitions are bidirectional, as the target and source models are always distinguished when defining the transformation rules.

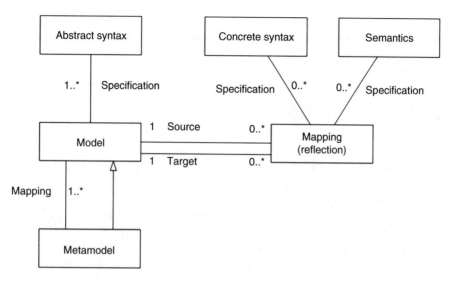

Fig. 3.3 Defining the DSL structure in a model-oriented way

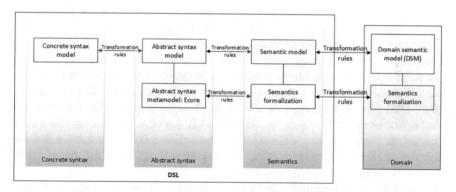

Fig. 3.4 Defining the DSL structure during cross-model transformation mechanisms

Additionally, all DSL levels can be specified by the user on the basis of the constructed models.

Structural concepts defined in a metamodel can be provided with a specific syntax by mapping them to corresponding (graphical or textual) symbols. The same concepts can also be provided with semantics by mapping them to a semantic domain such as membership equational logic (MEL) in Maude [61]. This logic is a highly heterogeneous Horne logic, whose atomic formulas are equations of the form $t = t'$ and $t : s$ asserting that t is a term of type s. This logic is very close to the taxonomy relation in ontologies and can be used to formalize it in the form of logical predicates.

Using these ideas, it can be argued that all the components of the DSL can be identified from the DSM and subsequent transformations between the different levels of the DSL structure using cross-model transformation mechanisms, which in our case are called projections (structural-semantic mappings in some other studies), as shown in Fig. 3.4.

3.6.2 Semantic DSL Model

Since a DSL is based on the subject field, at the semantic level, it contains concepts that are present in it [43]. As a consequence, if we can formalize a model of the domain, it is then possible to compare it with the semantic model of the DSL and make a judgment on the relevance of the DSL to the original domain. Moreover, such a formal model of the domain can also be used on the level of abstract language syntax, since it already contains the description of all necessary language entities.

From the point of view that the DSL corresponds to the target domain, users of the DSL can understand the meaning of language commands and expressions. However, in this case, it is more correct to speak of the semantics of the language as some model describing the objects of the domain and the relationships between them [34]. In this sense, the semantics of a language can be based on the semantic model of the domain [14].

In what follows, we will understand semantics as the set of rules for interpreting (mapping) the abstract syntax of the DSL in terms of a formal (semantic) model of the subject domain [41]. This is true from the point of view that we consider DSLs in the context of software systems whose description can be represented as a model (e.g., UML) that can be used as a basis for DSL development (in particular, the description of the set of objects used in DSLs). In our case, the denotational way of defining semantics is used to describe the semantics of DSLs (for a more detailed description of this and other ways of defining semantics, see [116]), described by Stoy [97], Strachey et al. [75], and Ershov [17, 32].

According to this approach, semantics is described in terms of functions (in our case, rules) which define correspondences between language syntax and semantic meaning (denotation) [97]. As stated in [115], according to this approach, we need to define several formal structures: R, the set of names used in the language; D, the range of values; $S = D^R = R \rightarrow D$, memory states during name processing; $[[P]] \subseteq S \rightarrow S = (R \rightarrow D) \rightarrow (R \rightarrow D)$, defining the meaning of the program in terms of the language; and $[[y]]_D : S \rightarrow D$, $[[x]]_R : S \rightarrow R$, $[[u]]_C : S \rightarrow \{0, 1\}$, defining values of algebraic, naming expressions and condition values, respectively.

At the same time, as noted in [17], the denotational way of defining the semantics of a language allows to reduce the representation of the semantics of a language to the following form: $DS : (P \times D \rightarrow D)$, where P is the program and D—data. In accordance with this statement, in the case of a DSL, language semantics can be specified by a set of rules transforming constructions of a particular DSL syntax (programs) to metamodel objects (data). These, in turn, are transformed through cross-model transformations to the level of the semantic model of the DSL and the semantic model of the domain.

3.6.3 Methods for Developing a DSL Metamodel

The abstract syntax of a language is usually described in the form of a metamodel that includes the basic concepts of the domain (language), the relationships between them, and a set of rules that specify the constraints on both the concepts and the relationships between them within the domain [33, 43].

In this sense, the abstract syntax (metamodel) of the DSL is presented as an artifact containing information about language objects and the relationships between them without specifying the behavioral aspects (i.e., the aspects of end user use of DSL constructs).

The selection of an abstract DSL syntax in this case is necessary in order to build the most complete DSL structure and to enable the modification of a specific DSL syntax independently of other levels of the DSL structure. Since the DSL metamodel contains only language objects and the links between them, this representation is independent of which type of DSL is used and makes it possible to implement various specific DSL syntaxes on the basis of a single metamodel. In this way, consistency between different DSL dialects is ensured, because conversions between them are possible at the level of abstract syntax.

However, we can also extend this metamodel according to changes in the semantic model of the DSL (and, by extension, the semantic model of the domain) without affecting the level of the specific syntax.

From a formal point of view, a DSL metamodel can be derived by projecting the set of objects of the target domain and operations on them. Given that any model is a combination of (E,R) of some set of entities and relations between them, the DSL metamodel can be formalized in a model-oriented form in the following form [44].

- **The set of metamodel entities** $E = \{e_i\}$, $i \in \mathbb{N}$, $i < \infty$ where each entity $e_i = \{SName_i, SICount_i, Attr_i, Opp_i, SRest_i\}$ is characterized by its name ($SName_i$ unique within the particular model), the allowed number of instances of the entity ($SICount_i \in \mathbb{N}$, $SICount_i \geq 0$), set of attributes ($Attr_i = \{attr_{j_i}\}$, $j_i \in \mathbb{N}$, $j_i < \infty$), a set of operations on entity instances ($Opp_i = \{opp_{j_i}\}$, $j_i \in \mathbb{N}$, $j_i < \infty$), and a set of constraints ($SRest_i = \{srest_{j_i}\}$, $j_i \in \mathbb{N}$, $j_i < \infty$).
- **The set of relations between entities** $R = \{r_i\}$, $i \in \mathbb{N}$, $i < \infty$ where each relationship $r_i = \{RName_i, RType_i, RMult_i, RRest_i\}$ is defined by its name ($RName_i$ unique within a particular model); type ($RType_i \in \mathbb{N}$, $RType_i \geq 0$) defined by the nature of the relation; multiplicity (or cardinality in the relation) ($RMult_i \in \mathbb{N}$, $RMult_i \geq 0$), which determines how many instances of entities involved in the relation can be used; and a set of constraints ($RRest_i = \{rrest_{j_i}\}$, $j_i \in \mathbb{N}$, $j_i < \infty$).

Based on these provisions, the structure of the DSL metamodel can be defined (E, R, $Rest$, Opp) where the first two elements E and Rel represent the object level and the remaining $Rest = \bigcup_{i=1}^{|E|} SRest_i \bigcup_{i=1}^{|E|} RRest_i$, Opp represent the functional aspects of the DSL. Interpreting a set of E as a set of entities in the domain, R as a set of relations between them, and Opp, $Rest$ as a set of operations on entities and constraints on them (respectively), it can be argued that the structure of the DSM (presented in Sect. 2.1) and the structure of the DSL metamodel correspond to each other. As a consequence, it is possible to organize an automated transformation between them through cross-model transformations. The only remaining issue is the implementation of such transformations at the level of the DSL syntax, which is discussed in the next section.

3.6.4 Methods for Modeling a Specific DSL Syntax

The concrete syntax of a DSL is a set of direct commands and expressions that determine the ability to access certain features of the DSL and, as a consequence, the subject domain. In this sense, a concrete language syntax is created by establishing correspondences between components of the abstract language syntax (metamodels) and their concrete representations in textual or graphical form. From this point of view, we can say that the concrete syntax of a DSL can be derived as some representation of its metamodel and defines the functional aspects of the DSL [64].

In the case of textual DSLs, the specific syntax of the language is defined by the grammar. A grammar is a set of rules that describe how a textual script of a DSL is turned into a syntax tree [40]. Each rule has some kind of header (non-terminal) and a body (output instruction). The grammar defines the structure of the syntax tree that is generated for a particular language, and it is possible to recognize several syntax trees for some fragment of source text in that language.

As shown in Sect. 2.2.2, the semantic level of the DSL can be fully described in a model-oriented way. In addition to this, a similar model-oriented representation of the syntactic part of the DSL has to be constructed [36]. In this case, we argue that objects on the syntactic level are projections of objects on the semantic level. Consequently, in this case, we obtain full equivalence of the semantic and syntactic levels of the DSL.

As a consequence, the syntactic level of the DSL can be formalized as a triplet $(O_{syntax}, R_{syntax}, Rule_{syntax})$ where $O_{syntax} \subseteq E$ and $R_{syntax} \subseteq R$ are subsets of sets of objects and relations between them of the metamodel of the DSL and $Rule_{syntax}$ is a set of rules describing mappings between the metamodel and a specific DSL syntax.

This definition of a specific DSL syntax based on its metamodel is independent of the type of specific DSL syntax (e.g., textual or visual) [103]. For visual languages, it is necessary to establish relationships between entities and the visual symbols that represent them, as is done, for example, with the Eclipse Graphical Modeling Framework (GMF) [29]. This is also true for textual languages, which require establishing links between metamodel elements and the syntactic structures of the textual DSL (e.g., those created with Xtext tools [113]).

Under these conditions, we can speak of a complete model-oriented representation of the DSL syntax structure. The structure allows not only to describe both levels of the DSL syntax in a structured and unified way but also to optimize the process of DSL design and further development by introducing several DSL syntactic dialects on one immutable metamodel. Moreover, the evolution of the DSL can be managed in a similar way both at the meta-level and at the level of a specific syntax, without having to re-create the whole structure of the DSL every time a change is required. This is important because a DSL can have several specific syntaxes combined by a single metamodel.

3.7 Formalization of Cross-Model Transformations Based on Graph Models

Before proceeding to formalize cross-model transformations, the source and target languages of the simulation need to be precisely defined. In our case, a combination of metamodeling techniques and graph transformations is used for this purpose: the static language structure is described by means of a metamodel unambiguously separating static and dynamic language concepts, while the dynamic operational semantics is defined by means of graph transformations.

A graph transformation is the result of manipulating a graph (in our case, a model) using some rules that are conceptually very similar to Chomsky well-known grammar rules, but using graph patterns instead of text patterns [2]. Formally, *a graph transformation rule* is a triple $Rule = (Lhs, Neg, Rhs)$ where Lhs is the left (source) graph (pattern), Rhs is the right (target) graph (of the model), and Neg (which is optional) describes a negative condition of application [8]. From an informal point of view, Lhs and Neg define *a precondition*, and Rhs defines *a postcondition* of the application of the relevant rule.

Applying a rule to a model (graph) M is to replace a pattern defined in the structure Lhs to the pattern defined in Rhs. This process can be described in more detail as (i) *searching for a match* with the pattern Lhs in the model M; (ii) *checking for a negative application condition* Neg which identifies the presence of forbidden elements in the model M (iii) *removing* a part of the model M (including deletion of a part of the model that may be matched to the template Neg, deletion of a part of the model that may be mapped to a template but not to the template Rhs, deletion of a part of the model that may be mapped to but not the template), thereby obtaining an intermediate model IM (iv) *adding* new elements to the intermediate model IM (v) adding new elements to the intermediate model that exist in the Rhs, but cannot be mapped into Lhs, giving a derived model M.

In this case, the graph transformation rules play the role of elementary operations, while the entire operational semantics of the language (model transformation) is determined by the model transformation system.

Since we describe the model transformation using the graph-oriented approach (see [77] for more details) in ATL transformation language, the procedure to derive the OCL invariants needs to be implemented. Using the principles of inductive invariants, we need to describe the correspondence between different components of the source and the target models.

This is fully consistent with the concept of the ATL transformation language. In this language, a bidirectional transformation consists of a set of relations between two models. There are two types of relations: top-level and non-top-level. The execution of a transformation requires that all its top-level relations hold, whereas non-top-level ones only need to hold when invoked directly or transitively from another relation [36].

Each relation defines two domain patterns, one for each model, and a pair of optional when and where OCL predicates. These optional predicates define the link with other relations in the transformation: the when clause indicates the constraints under which the relation needs to hold and the where clause provides additional conditions, apart from the ones expressed by the relation itself, that must be satisfied by all model elements in the relation.

Among all nodes in a domain pattern, one is marked as a root element. Definition of root nodes is purely for the sake of clarity that does not affect the semantics of the matching process. When referring to other relations in when or where clauses, parameters can be specified, and thus, it is possible to pass bound variables from one relation to another. Note that the bound objects received as parameters are necessary preconditions to enforce the pattern. According to these principles, when we talk about deriving the transformation system from the QVT transformation, we need to identify the invariants of both levels, top-relation and non-top-relation, to provide the whole consistence between the source and the target models. In what follows, we use OCL constraints to define the specific invariants of both types.

Definition 1 Let p be a top-relation with domain patterns $S = \{root_s, s_1, \ldots, s_n\}$ and $T = \{root_t, t_1, \ldots, t_m\}$ and $T_{when} \subseteq T$ be the set of elements of T referenced in p's "when" section. Then, the following top-relation invariant takes place for the $S \rightarrow T$:

$$\textbf{context } type\,(root_s) \textbf{ inv } p :$$
$$\left(\begin{array}{l} type(x_i)::allInstances() \rightarrow forAll(x_i| \\ type(x_j)::allInstances() \rightarrow forAll(x_j|... \end{array}\right) \forall x_k \in (S \backslash \{root_s\}) \cup T_{when}$$
$$\textbf{if } self.p - enabled\,(x_i, x_j, \ldots) \textbf{ then} \qquad (3.2)$$
$$\left(\begin{array}{l} type(x_u)::allInstances() \rightarrow exists(x_u| \\ type(x_v)::allInstances() \rightarrow exists(x_v|... \end{array}\right) \forall x_w \in T \backslash T_{when}$$
$$self.p - mapping\,(x_i, x_j, \ldots, x_u, x_v, \ldots) \ldots)) \textbf{ endif} \ldots))$$

$$\textbf{context } type\,(root_s) :: p - enabled(x_i : type\,(x_i), \ldots)$$
$$\textbf{body} : when\ and\ enabling\ conditions \qquad (3.3)$$

$$\textbf{context } type\,(root_s) :: p - mapping(x_i : type\,(x_i), \ldots)$$
$$\textbf{body} : where\ and\ mapping\ conditions \qquad (3.4)$$

Definition 2 Let p be a non-top-relation with domain patterns $S = \{root_s, s_1, \ldots, s_n\}$ and $T = \{root_t, t_1, \ldots, t_m\}$ and $T_{when} \subseteq T$ be the set of elements of T referenced in p's "when" section and $P = \{a_1, \ldots, a_k\} \subseteq S \cup T$ the set of elements passed as parameters in the call to p from other relations.

Then, the following non-top-relation invariant (a Boolean operation) takes place for the $S \rightarrow T$:

$$\text{context } type(root_s) :: p(a_1 : type(a_1), \ldots, a_k : type(a_k))$$
$$\left(\begin{matrix} type(x_i)::allInstances() \rightarrow forAll(x_i| \\ type(x_j)::allInstances() \rightarrow forAll(x_j|\ldots \end{matrix} \right) \forall x_k \in (S \backslash \{root_s\} \backslash P) \cup T_{when}$$
$$\textbf{if } self.p - enabled(x_i, x_j, \ldots) \textbf{ then}$$
$$\left(\begin{matrix} type(x_u)::allInstances() \rightarrow exists(x_u| \\ type(x_v)::allInstances() \rightarrow exists(x_v|\ldots \end{matrix} \right) \forall x_w \in T \backslash T_{when} \backslash P$$
$$self.p - mapping(x_i, x_j, \ldots, a_1, \ldots, a_k \ x_u, x_v, \ldots) \ldots)) \textbf{ endif} \ldots))$$

$$(3.5)$$

After such extraction of the invariants from the ATL transformations, the correctness of the model transformation can be applied for solving two problems [91]: (1) verification of correctness properties of transformations, that is, finding defects in them, and (2) validation of transformations, that is, identifying transformations whose definition does not match the designer intent.

With the application of OCL invariants, both problems can be solved using existing OCL verification and validation tools for the analysis of model transformations. With these inputs, verification tools provide means to automatically check the consistency of the transformation model without user intervention. Checking consistency allows the verification of the executability of the transformation and the use of all validation scenarios. Other properties checked automatically by OCL analysis tools (e.g., redundancy of an invariant) lead to the verification of other properties, chosen as a correctness property, described in the previous sections [90].

However, when it comes to creating a complete DSL structure, we cannot limit ourselves to a single transformation rule, as most often a DSL includes many concepts (entities) that have to be reflected in the target DSL metamodel (and in its structure as a whole). The question arises about the reusability of certain cross-model transformation rules and the validation of model (graph) transformations performed by them, which will be discussed in the next chapter.

3.8 Defining Rule-Based Model Transformations with Triple Graph Grammars

A directed unattributed graph [88] $G = (G_V, G_E, src, tar)$ consists of a set of vertices G_V, a set of edges G_E, a mapping $src : G_E \rightarrow G_V$ assigning to each edge a start vertex, and a mapping $tar : G_V \rightarrow G_E$ assigning to each edge a target vertex. A signature $\Sigma = \langle S, OP \rangle$ consists of a set of sort symbols S and a set of operation symbols OP. A Σ-algebra A is an S-indexed family $(A_s)_{s \in S}$ of carrier sets together with an OP-indexed family of mappings $(op^A)_{op \in OP}$ that contains for each $op : s_1 \ldots s_n \mapsto s$ a mapping $op^A : A_{s_1} \ldots A_{s_n} \mapsto A_s$. We denote by $|A|$ the disjoint union of the carrier sets A_s of A, for all $s \in S$, which is usually infinite.

An attributed graph AG where only graph vertices can be attributed is a pair consisting of a directed unlabeled graph G and a Σ-algebra A such that $|A| \subseteq G_V$.

The elements of $|A|$ represent potential attribute values which are regarded as special data vertices of the graph (besides the object vertices that model structural entities). An object vertex $v \in G_V$ has an attribute value $a \in |A|$ if there is an edge from v to a in AG.

An attributed type graph ATG is an attributed graph [91] where A is the final Σ-algebra having $A_s = \{s\}$ for all $s \in S$. An attributed instance graph is an attributed graph with an additional typing morphism which specifies the type of all vertices of the graph.

A *graph morphism* $f : G \rightarrow H$ is a pair of functions ($f_V : G_V \rightarrow H_V$, $f_E : G_E \rightarrow H_E$) compatible with the graph structure, preserving sources and targets: $f_V \circ s_G = s_H \circ f_E$ and $f_V \circ t_G = t_H \circ f_E$.

An *attributed graph morphism* $f : \langle G_1, A_1 \rangle \rightarrow \langle G_2, A_2 \rangle$ is a pair of a Σ-homomorphism $f_A = (f_s)_{s \in S} : A_1 \rightarrow A_2$ and a graph homomorphism $f_G = \langle f_V, f_E \rangle : G_1 \rightarrow G_2$ such that $|f_A| \subseteq f_V$, where $|f_A| = \bigcup_{s \in S} f_s$ and $A_{1s} = f_V^{-1}(A_{2s})$ for all $s \in S$. Informally, an attributed graph morphism preserves the graph structure of the attributed graphs [63].

Typed attributed graphs are manipulated by typed attributed graph transformation rules. A typed attributed graph transformation rule $r : L ::= R$ is composed of a rule name r and a pair of typed attributed graphs L and R. It fixes a set of variables X and is attributed over the term algebra $T_\Sigma(X)$, meaning that the graphs in the rule may have attribute values obtained from terms over variables in X. Using the well-known double-pushout approach [56], a morphism o is usually used for specifying the occurrence of a given rule r in a larger context within a graph G. The data type part is kept constant during transformation, i.e., modification of an attribute of an object vertex corresponds to deleting an edge from the object vertex to a data vertex and creating a new edge from the object to another data vertex.

A typed attributed graph transformation system $GTS = (\Sigma, ATG, X, \mathcal{R})$ consists of a data type signature Σ, an attributed type graph ATG, a family of variables X over Σ, and a set of attributed graph transformation rules $\mathcal{R}$ over ATG and X [63]. The rules induce a relation on the set of graphs. One writes $G \overset{r(o)}{\Rightarrow} H$ to denote that graph H is derived from graph G by applying the rule $r \in R$ at occurrence o. A transformation sequence $G_0 \overset{*}{\Rightarrow} G_n = G_0 \overset{r_1(o_1)}{\Rightarrow} \ldots \overset{r_n(o_n)}{\Rightarrow} G_n$ in GTS is a sequence of consecutive transformation steps such that all rules r_i are from $\mathcal{R}$. To abbreviate, we also write $G \overset{r}{\Rightarrow} H$ for $G \overset{r(o)}{\Rightarrow} H$.

After the definition of graph transformation and corresponding rules are given, we can reflect these concepts on more general triple graph grammars (TGGs). TGGs were proposed by A. Schürr [91] as a formal means to specify transformations between two languages in a declarative way. TGGs are founded on the notion of graph grammar. A graph grammar is made of rules having graphs in their left- and right-hand sides (LHS and RHS), plus the initial graph to be transformed. Applying a rule to a graph is only possible if an occurrence of the LHS (a match) is found in it. Once such occurrence is found, it is replaced by the RHS graph. This is called direct derivation. It may be possible to find several matches for a rule, and then one is chosen at random. The execution of a grammar is also non-deterministic: at each step, one rule is randomly chosen, and its application is tried. The execution ends when no rule can be applied.

Even though graph grammar rules rely on pre- and postconditions, and on pattern matching, when used for model-to-model transformation, they have an operational, unidirectional style, as the rules specify how to build the target model assuming the source already exists. On the contrary, TGGs are declarative and bidirectional since, starting from a unique TGG specifying the synchronized evolution of two graphs, it is possible to generate forward and backward transformations as well as operational mechanisms for other scenarios.

TGGs are made of rules working on triple graphs. These are made of two graphs called source and target, related through a correspondence graph. Any kind of graph can be used for these three components, from standard unattributed graphs $(V; E; s, t : E \rightarrow V)$ to more complex attributed graphs, e.g., e-graphs. The nodes in the correspondence graph (the mappings) have morphisms to the nodes in the source and target graphs. Triple morphisms are defined as three graph morphisms that preserve the correspondence functions. They are used to relate the LHS and RHS of a TGG rule, to identify a match of the LHS in a graph, and to type a triple graph.

Triple Graph and Morphism [100] A triple graph is made of two graphs G_S and G_t called source and target, related through the nodes of the correspondence graph $G_C : TrG = \left(G_S, G_C, G_t, cs : V_{G_C} \rightarrow V_{G_S}, ct : V_{G_C} \rightarrow V_{G_t}\right)$.

A triple graph morphism $f = (f_S, f_C, f_t) : TrG^1 \rightarrow TrG^2$ is made of three graph morphisms $f_x : G_x^1 \rightarrow G_x^2$ (with $x = \{s, c, t\}$) such that the correspondence functions are preserved [108].

Here, V_{G_x} is the set of nodes of graph G_x. Morphisms cs and ct relate two nodes x and y in the source and target graphs iff $\exists n \in V_{G_C}$ with $cs(n) = x$ and $ct(n) = y$. A triple graph can be depicted by $\langle G_S, G_C, G_t \rangle$ and TrG_x (for $x = \{s, c, t\}$) to refer to the x component of TrG. In this way, $\langle G_S, G_C, G_t \rangle_s = G_S$.

A triple graph is typed by a metamodel triple or TGG schema, which contains the source and target metamodels and declares allowed mappings between both [100]. A typed triple graph is formally represented as $(TrG, type : TrG \rightarrow MM)$, where the first element is a triple graph and the second a morphism to the metamodel triple. Morphisms between typed triple graphs must respect the typing morphism and can take inheritance into account, as in [36].

For simplicity of presentation, we omit the typing in the following definitions. Besides a metamodel triple, a M2M transformation by TGGs consists of a set of declarative rules that describe the synchronized evolution of two models. Rules have triple graphs in their LHS and RHS and may include OCL attribute conditions. This contrasts with the usual approach of using attribute computations in the rules instead of conditions [39]. We use the latter as it poses some benefits that will be shown later on when operationalizing the rules. Declarative rules are non-deleting because they describe how models are created; hence, they are defined by an injective triple morphism.

Declarative TGG Rule [112] A declarative TGG rule $p = (r : L \rightarrow R, ATT_{COND})$ is made of two triple graphs, $L = \langle L_S, L_C, L_t \rangle$ and $R = \langle R_S, R_C, R_t \rangle$, an injective triple morphism r between L and R, and a set ATT_{COND} of OCL constraints over R, expressing attribute conditions.

A TGG is bidirectional as rules do not specify any direction, but synchronously create and relate source and target elements. A TGG defines the language of all triple graphs that satisfy the metamodel constraints and that can be derived using zero or more applications of the grammar rules. Please note that some derived graphs may not conform to the metamodel and hence are not part of the language.

In practice, no one uses declarative TGG rules to create source and target models at the same time, as it would require a synchronous coupling of both models. Instead, so-called operational rules are derived for different tasks, e.g., to perform forward (source-to-target) and backward (target-to-source) transformations.

A forward transformation creates a set of target elements that correspond to a given set of initial source model elements and conversely with a backward transformation. The algorithm to derive such rules was proposed in [89] for the description of operational rules for other purposes.

Operational TGG Rule [91] The following operational rules can be derived, given the declarative TGG rule $p = (r : L = \langle L_S, L_C, L_t \rangle \rightarrow R = \langle R_S, R_C, R_t \rangle, ATT_{COND})$:

- Forward: $\overrightarrow{p} = (r' : \langle R_S, L_C, L_t \rangle \rightarrow \langle R_S, R_C, R_t \rangle, \overrightarrow{ATT}_{LHS}, \overrightarrow{ATT}_{RHS})$
- Backward: $\overleftarrow{p} = (r' : \langle L_S, L_C, R_t \rangle \rightarrow \langle R_S, R_C, R_t \rangle, \overleftarrow{ATT}_{LHS}, \overleftarrow{ATT}_{RHS})$

where $\overrightarrow{ATT}_{LHS}$ (resp., $\overleftarrow{ATT}_{LHS}$) contains the part of the ATT_{COND} OCL expression concerning elements of the LHS of the forward (resp., backward) operational rule only. $\overrightarrow{ATT}_{RHS}$ (resp., $\overleftarrow{ATT}_{RHS}$) contains the part of ATT_{COND} not included in $\overrightarrow{ATT}_{LHS}$ (resp., $\overleftarrow{ATT}_{LHS}$).

The operational rules enforce the pattern given by the declarative rule; thus, their RHS is equal to the RHS of the declarative rule. In the forward case, the LHS assumes that the source graph already exists, whereas in the backward case, the existence of the target graph is assumed. In the rest of the chapter, we use L_F and L_B to refer to the LHS of the forward and backward rules. The conditions in ATT_{COND} are split in those to be checked on the LHS before ($\overrightarrow{ATT}_{RHS}$ *and* $\overleftarrow{ATT}_{RHS}$) and those to be checked after rule application ($\overrightarrow{ATT}_{RHS}$ and $\overleftarrow{ATT}_{RHS}$).

3.9   Definition of GTS Using Invariants

In the previous section, we introduced the definition of model transformations using graph-oriented mechanisms (especially, TGG and graph transformation rules). We also mentioned that any graph transformation rule contains the negative application rule, which defines the inability to provide corresponding graph transformation.

Such a negative rule informally can be described as follows: we try to check if the source graph structure satisfies some structural pattern (in part of objects, etc.). From this point of view, the process of graph transformation resembles the search for various structural invariants in the source target with consequent application of corresponding graph transformation rules to them. In order to demonstrate this idea more precisely, we can reformulate model transformations using some invariant technics.

Graph Conditions [58, 63] Nested graph conditions generalize the corresponding notions, where a negative (positive) application condition, NAC (PAC) for short, over a graph P, denoted $\neg\exists a(\exists a)$, is defined in terms of a graph morphism. We use $\rightarrow$ to denote a graph morphism in general and $\hookrightarrow$ to denote an injective graph morphism in particular. Informally, a morphism $p : P \rightarrow G$ satisfies $\neg\exists a(\exists a)$ if there does not exist a morphism $q : C \rightarrow G$ extending p (if there exists q extending p). Then, a *(nested) graph condition AC* is either the special condition true or a pair of the form $\neg\exists(a, ac_C)$ or $\exists(a, ac_C)$, where the first case corresponds to a NAC and the second to a PAC and in both cases ac_C is an additional AC on C. Intuitively, a morphism $p : P \rightarrow G$ satisfies $\exists(a, ac_C)$ if p satisfies a and the corresponding extension q satisfies ac_C. ACs (and also NACs and PACs) may be combined with the usual logical connectors. A morphism $p : P \rightarrow G$ satisfies $\neg c$ if p does not satisfy c and satisfies $\bigwedge_{i \in I} c_i$ if it satisfies each c_i ($i \in I$).

Graph conditions over the empty graph I are also called *graph constraints*. A graph G satisfies a graph constraint ac_I, written $G \vDash ac_I$, if the initial morphism $i_G : I \rightarrow G$ satisfies ac_I. This means that if a constraint simply should state that a match for a graph C must exist, we have the graph constraint $\exists(i_C, true)$.

Notation   Note that $\exists a$ abbreviates $\exists(a, true)$, $\forall(a, ac_C)$ abbreviates $\neg\exists(a, \neg ac_C)$, and $\exists(i_C, ac_C)$ with the initial morphism $i_C : I \rightarrow C$ abbreviates $\exists(C, ac_C)$.

Graph Transformation and Invariants   In what follows, we assume the double-pushout approach (DPO) to graph transformation with injective matching [63]. A *plain* rule $p = \langle L \hookleftarrow I \hookrightarrow R \rangle$ consists of a left-hand side (LHS) L and a right-hand side (RHS). Additionally, we allow rules to be equipped with LHS application conditions, allowing to apply a given rule to a graph G only if the corresponding match morphism satisfies the AC of the rule. Thus, a *rule* $\rho = \langle p, ac_L \rangle$ consists of a *plain* rule $p = \langle L \hookleftarrow I \hookrightarrow R \rangle$ and an application condition ac_L over L.

A *direct transformation* via rule $\rho = \langle p, ac_L \rangle$ consists of two pushouts (1) and (2), called DPO, with injective match m and comatch m^* such that $m \vDash ac_L$. If there exists a direct transformation from G to G' via rule ρ and match m, we write $G \Longrightarrow_{m,\rho} G'$. If we are only interested in the rule ρ, we write $G \Longrightarrow_\rho G'$. If a rule ρ in a set of rules $\mathcal{R}$ exists such that there exists a direct transformation via rule ρ from G to G', we write $G \Longrightarrow_{\mathcal{R}} G'$. A *graph transformation*, denoted as $G_0 \overset{*}{\Longrightarrow}_{\mathcal{R}} G_n$, is a sequence $G_0 \Longrightarrow_{\mathcal{R}} G_1 \Longrightarrow_{\mathcal{R}} \cdots \Longrightarrow_{\mathcal{R}} G_n$ of $n \geq 1$ direct transformations [63].

Graph conditions, rules, and transformations as described before can be equipped with *typing* over a given type graph TG as usual by adding typing morphisms from each graph to TG and by requiring type compatibility with respect to TG for each graph morphism. We denote with $\mathcal{L}(TG)$ the set of all graphs G typed over TG.

Graph Transformation System [58, 63] A graph transformation system (GTS) $gts = (\mathcal{R}, TG)$ consists of a set of rules $\mathcal{R}$ typed over a type graph TG. A graph transformation system may be equipped with an initial graph G_0 or a set of initial graphs I being graphs typed over TG. For a GTS $gts = (\mathcal{R}, TG)$ and a set of initial graphs I, the set of reachable graphs $REACH(gts, I)$ is defined as $\{G \mid G_0 \overset{*}{\Longrightarrow}_{\mathcal{R}} G, G_0 \in I\}$.

The applicability of a rule can be expressed as a graph constraint. The rule applicability constraint for a rule $\rho = \langle p, ac_L \rangle$ with $p = \left(L \overset{l}{\hookleftarrow} I \overset{r}{\hookrightarrow} R \right)$ expresses that an injective match m exists such that the application condition ac_L and the so-called deletable condition $Deletable(p)$, guaranteeing the existence of a PO complement for $m \circ l$, are fulfilled. Then it is obvious that the rule $\rho = \langle p, ac_L \rangle$ is applicable with injective matching to a graph G if and only if G fulfills the rule applicability constraint.

Rule Applicability Constraint Given a rule $\rho = \langle p, ac_L \rangle$ with plain rule $p = \langle L \hookleftarrow I \hookrightarrow R \rangle$, then $App(\rho) = \exists(i_L, ac_L \bigwedge Deletable(p))$ is the rule applicability constraint of ρ.

The satisfaction of graph constraints can be invariant with respect to a GTS.

Inductive Invariant A graph constraint ac_I is an inductive invariant of the GTS $gts = (\mathcal{R}, TG)$, if for all graphs G in $\mathcal{L}(TG)$, and for all rules $\rho \in R$, it holds that $G \vDash ac_I \wedge G \Longrightarrow_\rho G'$ implies $G' \vDash ac_I$.

Triple Graph Grammars Triple graph grammars (TGGs) [58, 63] define model transformations in a relational (declarative) way. We use a TGG formalization by Golas as more suitable for the current practice for TGGs than the one introduced originally by Shur. Thereby, the main idea is to use a distinguished, fixed graph $TRIPLE$ which all triple graphs, including the type triple graph $S_{TT} C_{TT} T_{TT}$, are typed over.

We say that $TRIPLE_S$, $TRIPLE_C$, and $TRIPLE_T$ are the *source, correspondence*, and *target component* of $TRIPLE$, respectively.

Analogous to the aforementioned case, the projection of a graph G typed over $TRIPLE$ to $TRIPLE_S$, $TRIPLE_C$, or $TRIPLE_T$ selects the corresponding component of this graph.

We denote a triple graph as a combination of three indexed capitals, as, for example, $G = S_G C_G T_G$, where S_G denotes the *source* and T_G denotes the *target component* of G, while C_G denotes the *correspondence component*, being the smallest subgraph of G such that all c-nodes as well as all e_{cs}- and e_{ct}-edges are included in C_G. Note that C_G has to be a proper graph, i.e., all target nodes of e_{cs}- and e_{ct}-edges have to be included. The category of triple graphs and triple graph morphisms is called **TripleGraphs**.

Analogous to typed graphs, *typed triple graphs* are triple graphs typed over a distinguished triple graph $S_{TT}C_{TT}T_{TT}$, called type triple graph. The category of typed triple graphs and morphisms is called **TripleGraphs$_{TT}$**. In what follows, we assume every triple graph $S_G C_G T_G$ and triple graph morphism f to be typed over $S_{TT}C_{TT}T_{TT}$, even if not explicitly mentioned. In particular, this means that S_G is typed over S_{TT}, C_G is typed over C_{TT}, and T_G is typed over T_{TT}. We say that S_G (T_G or C_G) is a *source graph* (*target graph* or *correspondence graph*, respectively) belonging to the language $\mathcal{L}(S_{TT})$ ($\mathcal{L}(T_{TT})$ or $\mathcal{L}(C_{TT})$, respectively).

Notation Note that each source graph (target graph) corresponds uniquely to a triple graph with empty correspondence and target (source and correspondence) components, respectively. Therefore, if it is clear from the context that we are dealing with triple graphs, we denote triple graphs $S_G \varnothing \varnothing$ ($\varnothing \varnothing T_G$) with empty correspondence and target components (source components) also as S_G (T_G), respectively.

A *triple graph rule* $p : S_L C_L T_L \xrightarrow{\ r\ } S_R C_R T_R$ consists of a triple graph morphism r, which is an inclusion. A *direct triple graph transformation* $S_G C_G T_G \Longrightarrow_{p,m} S_H C_H T_H$ from $S_G C_G T_G$ to $S_H C_H T_H$ via p and m consists of the pushout (*PO*) in **TripleGraphs$_{TT}$** [91].

A *triple graph transformation*, denoted as $S_{G_0} C_{G_0} T_{G_0} \overset{*}{\Longrightarrow} S_{G_n} C_{G_n} T_{G_n}$, is a sequence $S_{G_0} C_{G_0} T_{G_0} \Longrightarrow S_{G_1} C_{G_1} T_{G_1} \Longrightarrow \ldots \Rightarrow S_{G_n} C_{G_n} T_{G_n}$ of direct triple graph transformations. As in the context of classical triple graphs, we consider triple graph grammars (TGGs) with non-deleting rules. Moreover, we allow grammars to be equipped with a so-called TGG constraint $\lfloor_{tgg}$ typed over $S_{TT}C_{TT}T_{TT}$, restricting the language of triple graphs generated by the TGG to a subset of triple graphs satisfying $\lfloor_{tgg}$.

Triple Graph Grammar $\mathfrak{L}(tgg, \lfloor_{tgg})$ A triple graph grammar (TGG) $tgg = ((\mathcal{R}, S_{TT}C_{TT}T_{TT}), S_A C_A T_A)$ consists of a set of triple graph rules $\mathcal{R}$ typed over $S_{TT}C_{TT}T_{TT}$ and a triple start graph $S_A C_A T_A$, called axiom, also typed over $S_{TT}C_{TT}T_{TT}$. Given a TGG constraint $\lfloor_{tgg}$ for tgg, being a graph constraint typed over $S_{TT}C_{TT}T_{TT}$ such that $S_A C_A T_A \models \lfloor_{tgg}$, then the triple graph language $\mathfrak{L}(tgg, \lfloor_{tgg})$ consists of $S_A C_A T_A$ and all triple graphs $S_G C_G T_G \models \lfloor_{tgg}$ such that

$$S_A C_A T_A \overset{*}{\Longrightarrow} S_G C_G T_G \text{ via rules in } \mathcal{R}.$$

3.10   Behavior Preservation for Model Transformations

Assuming that a model transformation is defined by some relation over the source and target language, we can formulate the general problem of behavior preservation on the transformation level as follows:

Problem Statement (Behavior Preservation) [58, 63]   Given a model transformation $MT \subseteq \mathcal{L}(S_{TT}) \times \mathcal{L}(T_{TT})$ and operational semantic definitions sem_S and sem_T for source and target language $\mathcal{L}(S_{TT})$ and $\mathcal{L}(T_{TT})$, respectively, we say that MT is behavior preserving if for each pair of source and target graphs $(S, T) \in MT$, it holds that sem_S of S is somehow equivalent to sem_T of T.

In this case, the model transformation $MT \subseteq \mathcal{L}(S_{TT}) \times \mathcal{L}(T_{TT})$ is derived in our case from a given TGG tgg typed over $S_{TT}C_{TT}T_{TT}$. Additionally, tgg is allowed to be equipped with a TGG constraint $\lfloor_{tgg}$ such that MT can be derived from the language $\mathfrak{L}(tgg, \lfloor_{tgg})$.

Notion on $MT(tgg, \lfloor_{tgg})$ **[100]**   Given a TGG tgg with TGG constraint $\lfloor_{tgg}$, $MT(tgg, \lfloor_{tgg}) \subseteq \mathcal{L}(S_{TT}) \times \mathcal{L}(T_{TT})$ consists of pairs of source and target graphs (S, T) such that there exists some triple graph $SCT \in \mathfrak{L}(tgg, \lfloor_{tgg})$ having S and T as source and target component, respectively.

Analogous to the work of Hulschbusch et al. [50], we define the operational semantics sem_S and sem_T of source models and target models as graph transformation systems gts_S and gts_t, respectively. In order to be able to encode runtime information into the source and target language $\mathcal{L}(S_{TT})$ and $\mathcal{L}(T_{TT})$, the according type graphs can be enriched with so-called runtime types allowing to define the operational semantics of both languages as the possible changes in instances of this enhanced type graph (similar to the dynamic metamodeling approach). We denote these enhanced type graphs for the source (target) language as S_{RT} (T_{RT}), respectively. Accordingly, the type graph $S_{TT}C_{TT}T_{TT}$ enriched with runtime types for source and target languages is denoted as $S_{RT}C_{RT}T_{RT}$. In this context, we say that a type (or corresponding instance element) is *static* if it belongs to $S_{TT}C_{TT}T_{TT}$. We assume that operational semantic rules have the property that they do not change elements with static type, since they merely model the change of runtime information. Note that if some graph $S_G C_G T_G$, morphism m, rule ρ, or condition ac is typed over a subgraph $S_{SG}C_{SG}T_{SG}$ of $S_{RT}C_{RT}T_{RT}$, then it is straightforward to extend the codomain of the corresponding typing morphisms to $S_{RT}C_{RT}T_{RT}$ such that $S_G C_G T_G$, m, ac, or ρ are actually typed over $S_{RT}C_{RT}T_{RT}$.

Taking into account ideas above on the structural and inductive invariants, we can state that in this case, static types of graph components belong to the inductive invariants, since they are stable during the graph transformations. From this point of view, we can state that when we realize the transformation between the metamodel of a DSL and its syntactic dialects, we organize the inductive invariants.

Notion on gts_S **and** gts_t Given a source and target enhanced type graph S_{RT} and T_{RT}, respectively, we have a source GTS $gts_S = (\mathcal{R}_S = \{\rho_S^i | i \in I\}, S_{RT})$ for the source language $\mathcal{L}(S_{TT})$ and a target GTS $gts_t = (\mathcal{R}_t = \{\rho_t^j | j \in J\}, T_{RT})$ for the target language $\mathcal{L}(T_{TT})$, consisting of rules that preserve all elements with static type.

Finally, we also have to define what it means for two operational semantics to be somehow equivalent. For behavioral models that describe a reactive behavior, the external visible interactions rather than the usually encapsulated states are relevant. This can be captured by considering the labeled transition systems induced by the source and target GTS, where the labeling describes the externally visible interactions, defined by the corresponding rule names leading to operational semantics rule applications.

Notion on **Induced LTS(gts,G_0)** A labeled transition system (LTS) $lts = \langle i, \rightarrow, Q, L \rangle$ consists of the initial state i, the labeled transition relation $\rightarrow \subseteq Q \times L \times Q$ over the label alphabet L, and the set of states Q. Given a relabeling mapping $l : L \rightarrow L'$ with L' a new label alphabet, then $l(lts)$ is the labeled transition system where each label α in lts has been replaced by $l(\alpha)$. The labeled transition system $LTS(gts, G_0)$ induced by $gts = (\mathcal{R}, TG)$ and the initial graph G_0 equals $\langle G_0, \rightarrow_{gts}, Q_{gts}, \mathcal{R} \rangle$ with $\rightarrow_{gts} = \{(G, \rho, G') | G, G' \in Q_{gts}, \rho \in \mathcal{R} \wedge G \Rightarrow_\rho G'\}$ and $Q_{gts} = REACH(gts, \{G_0\})$.

Given two relabeling mappings $l_s : \mathcal{R}_S \rightarrow A$ and $l_t : \mathcal{R}_t \rightarrow A$ for $LTS(gts_s, S)$ and $LTS(gts_t, T)$, respectively, we can then obtain two transition systems $l_s(LTS(gts_s, S))$ and $l_t(LTS(gts_t, T))$ over a common alphabet A.

Now we can compare source and target behavior looking only at the labeling of transitions by requiring that a source S and target graph T have bisimilar LTSs $l_s(LTS(gts_s, S))$ and $l_t(LTS(gts_t, T))$. Bisimilarity of two LTSs over the same alphabet is defined as follows:

Notion on Bisimulation Relation (Bisimilarity) [58, 63] A bisimulation relation between two labeled transition systems $lts_1 = \langle i_1, \rightarrow, Q_1, A \rangle$ and $lts_2 = \langle i_2, \rightarrow, Q_2, A \rangle$ over the same alphabet A is a relation $B \subseteq Q_1 \times Q_2$ such that whenever $(q_1, q_2) \in B$:

1. If $q_1 \overset{\alpha}{\rightarrow} q'_1$, then $q_2 \overset{\alpha}{\rightarrow} q'_2$ and $(q'_1, q'_2) \in B$

2. If $q_2 \overset{\alpha}{\rightarrow} q'_2$, then $q_1 \overset{\alpha}{\rightarrow} q'_1$ and $(q'_1, q'_2) \in B$

We say that lts_1 and lts_2 are bisimilar if there exists a bisimulation relation between them such that $(i_1, i_2) \in B$.

Notion on Induced Bisimulation Relation $Bis(\lfloor_{Bis}, SCT)$ **[58, 63]** Given a pair of source and target graphs (S, T) in $MT(tgg)$ such that the triple graph SCT typed over $S_{TT}C_{TT}T_{TT}$ belongs to $\mathfrak{L}(tgg, \lfloor_{tgg})$ with two LTSs $l_s(LTS(gts_s, S))$ and $l_t(LTS(gts_t, T))$, and given a graph constraint $\lfloor_{Bis}$ typed over $S_{RT}C_{RT}T_{RT}$, called the bisimulation constraint, then the induced bisimulation relation $Bis(\lfloor_{Bis}, SCT) \subseteq REACH(gts_s, S) \times REACH(gts_t, T)$ consists of all (S', T') such that $S'CT'$ fulfills $\lfloor_{Bis}$.

Notion on Pairwise Constraint $\lfloor_{Pair}$, **Set of Parallel Rules** $\mathcal{P}(l_s, l_t)$ Given $gts_s = (\mathcal{R}_S, S_{RT})$ and $gts_t = (\mathcal{R}_t, T_{RT})$ as well as the relabeling mappings $l_s : \mathcal{R}_S \to A$ and $l_t : \mathcal{R}_t \to A$, the pairwise constraint

$$\lfloor_{Pair} = \wedge_{(\rho_s, \rho_t)}((App\,(\rho_s) \implies App\,(\rho_t)) \wedge (App\,(\rho_t) \implies App\,(\rho_s)))$$

typed over $S_{RT}C_{RT}T_{RT}$ with the set of pairs $Pair\,(l_s, l_t) = \{(\rho_s, \rho_t)\,|l_s\,(\rho_s) = l_t\,(\rho_t) \wedge \rho_s \in \mathcal{R}_S, \rho_t \in \mathcal{R}_t\}$. We define $\mathcal{P}\,(l_s, l_t) = \{\rho_s + \rho_t\,|(\rho_s, \rho_t) \in Pair\,(l_s, l_t)\}$ as the set of parallel rules induced by $Pair\,(l_s, l_t)$.

Behavior Preservation Verification Theorem (Proof Based on H. Giese and L. Lambers) Given a model transformation $MT\,(tgg, \lfloor_{tgg}) : \mathcal{L}\,(S_{TT}) \times \mathcal{L}\,(T_{TT})$ for a $tgg = ((\mathcal{R}, S_{TT}C_{TT}T_{TT}\,), S_A C_A T_A)$ with TGG constraint $\lfloor_{tgg}$; operational semantic definitions $gts_s = (\mathcal{R}_s, S_{RT})$ and $gts_t = (\mathcal{R}_t, T_{RT})$ for source and target language $\mathcal{L}\,(S_{TT})$ and $\mathcal{L}\,(T_{TT})$, respectively; relabeling mappings $l_s : \mathcal{R}_S \to A$ and $l_t : \mathcal{R}_t \to A$; and a bisimulation constraint $\lfloor_{Bis} = \lfloor_{Rt} \wedge \lfloor_{Pair} \wedge \lfloor_{tgg}$ typed over $S_{RT}C_{TT}T_{RT}$ with $\lfloor_{Rt}$ a given runtime constraint and $\lfloor_{Pair}$ the pairwise constraint, then $MT\,(tgg, \lfloor_{tgg})$ is behavior preserving if the following conditions are fulfilled:

1. $S_A C_A T_A \vDash \lfloor_{Rt} \wedge \lfloor_{Pair}$.
2. $\lfloor_{Rt} \wedge \lfloor_{Pair}$ is an inductive invariant of $(\mathcal{R}, S_{RT}C_{TT}T_{RT}\,)$.
3. $\lfloor_{Rt} \wedge \lfloor_{Pair}$ is an inductive invariant of $(\mathcal{P}\,(l_s, l_t)\,, S_{RT}C_{TT}T_{RT}\,)$ with $\mathcal{P}\,(l_s, l_t)$ as given above.

This theorem is the fundamental statement for applying cross-model transformations in the process of evolution of domain-specific languages and maintaining consistency of language dialects, which will be discussed later.

Overall Conclusion In summary, this chapter proposes a generalized model-oriented structure of the DSL and the formalisms required for it, including cross-model transformations.

To ensure the consistency of the DSL with the domain, it is proposed to use the conceptual (ontological) model of the domain. This also allows not to create the DSL structure from scratch manually, but to use the results of the domain analysis expressed as a formal artifact.

Cross-model transformations are used to organize transitions between different models (DSM, models of different levels of DSL structure). In this case, the essential characteristics (properties) of models and their objects (e.g., the property of belonging of an object to a certain class) are preserved during transformations.

In contrast to existing options for describing the structure of DSLs (in particular textual [48, 98] and visual [41]) reflecting either the abstract syntax of the DSL or the concrete syntax of the DSL, without reflecting the semantic aspects, the presented generalized structure allows to describe any DSL, regardless of its type, and allows to eliminate the drawbacks of the classical approach to DSL development discussed in Chap. 1, in particular by allowing to transfer results of the domain analysis stage to the direct DSL development stage by applying cross-model transformations to the DSM. Further, similar transformations can be used to construct all levels of the DSL syntax. This makes it possible to organize coordinated changes in the DSM and in the structure of the DSL.

A detailed description of the proposed approach to the development of DSLs based on the identified generalized DSL structure and cross-model transformations is presented in the next chapter.

Part II
A Projection Approach to DSL Development

Chapter 4
Developing a Projection Approach to DSL Development

Abstract This chapter proposes the author's solution to the problem posed in Chap. 2 of developing a generalized model of DSL evolution through cross-model transformations. In this case, we are talking about a chain of interrelated transformations, starting from the ontological DSM and ending with a model of a concrete DSL syntax. The generalized mathematical model, corresponding algorithms, and software tools are collectively referred to as the projection approach to DSL development.

4.1 Outline of the Proposed Projection Approach Based on a Generalized Model-Oriented DSL Structure and Cross-Model Transformations

Based on the object-oriented descriptions of the different levels of the DSL structure outlined in Sect. 2.3, and taking into account the possibility of defining model transformations using cross-model transformation rules while retaining essential features (properties) of models, we can argue that each individual fragment of the DSL, namely, semantics and abstract and concrete syntax, can be represented in a model-oriented form.

In this case, the semantics of the DSL is entirely based on the semantic model of the subject domain and can be described by means of an appropriate DSM. From this point of view, the semantics of DSLs can be described as a triplet $Sem = (O, R, A)$ where O is a set of objects of the domain; R, a set of relations between them; and A, the set of constraints of the domain (both on objects and on the relations between them).

A metamodel (abstract syntax) of a DSL can be represented as a set of $MM = (E, Rel, Rest, Opp)$ where the first two elements E and Rel represent the object level and the remaining $Rest = \bigcup_{i=1}^{|E|} SRest_i \bigcup_{i=1}^{|E|} RRest_i$, Opp represent functional aspects of the DSL. In contrast to other existing ways of representing the DSL metamodel (e.g., in accordance with the ideas of J. Luoma of [68]), in this case, we get a complete object-oriented representation at the metamodel level, with the possibility of transforming it to the level of a specific syntax.

The specific syntax can be formalized as a triplet $CS = (O_{syntax},\ R_{syntax})$ where $O_{syntax} \subseteq E$ and $R_{syntax} \subseteq R$ are subsets of the sets of objects and the relations between them of the DSL metamodel.

Given that any model is described by a pair of $(E,\ R)$ of some set of entities and a set of relationships between them, we can argue that the whole structure of the DSL can be represented in a model-oriented form.

As a consequence, transitions can be organized between DSM and models describing the semantic level of the DSL, the abstract syntax level and the concrete syntax level, using the cross-model transformations described in Sect. 2.4 (Fig. 4.1). By denoting $Rule_{sem}$, $Rule_{MM}$, and $Rule_{syntax}$, respectively, the rules of transition from DSM to model of semantics of a DSL, from model of semantics of a DSL to model of abstract syntax (metamodel) of a DSL, and from metamodel of a DSL to model of concrete syntax, we can state that structure of a DSL in model-oriented form is a set: $(Sem, Rule_{sem}, MM, Rule_{MM}, CS, Rule_{syntax})$.

In this case (Fig. 4.1), the result of applying transformation rules to a DSM to obtain a semantic model of the DSL is called a projection. The DSL metamodel derived from each individual projection through the application of appropriate transformation rules constitutes the syntax of the language. Finally, models of a particular syntax derived from a metamodel by applying appropriate transformation rules are different dialects of the DSL because they are based on a single metamodel and, consequently, contain different representations for the same objects and operations on them.

On this basis, the following new hierarchy of the DSL development process is proposed according to the projection approach (Fig. 4.2). In our case, this hierarchy

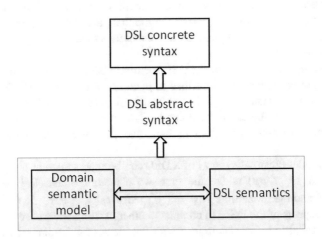

Fig. 4.1 Proposed approach to DSL development

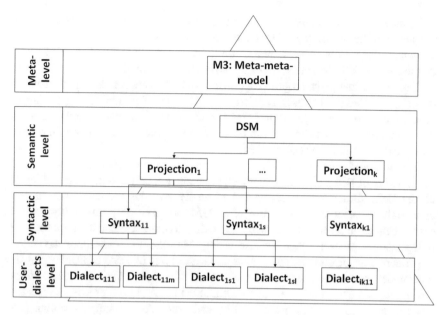

Fig. 4.2 Semantic hierarchy of the DSL development process in the projection approach

is divided into four levels according to the stages of DSL development. Each lower level is based on the model artifacts of the upper level [103].

Single meta-metamodel (kernel meta-metamodel, KM3 [49]) defines a common basis for all metamodels and lower-level models. The semantic hierarchy structure defines an appropriate process for the creation of external DSLs for the modeling of human-machine interfaces of general-purpose software systems. It begins with the definition of a DSM containing all the key objects of the target domain and the relationships between them. In this case, ontological models (domain ontologies) are used as DSM. It is important to note that within the framework of the approach, both completely new and already existing domain ontologies can be used. This is achieved due to the implementation of transformations (projections) at the level of the metamodel and not a specific DSM.

When the DSM has been created, we can construct a semantic model of the DSL using a semantic projection operation. Any semantic projection performs a certain M2M transformation of the DSM into some fragment of it. Thus, the semantic projection completely defines the semantic model of this or that dialect of DSL. In this case, the semantic model becomes an object-time structure, as it must be adapted according to changes in the DSM over time, thereby defining a new occupancy of the DSL object.

Once the result of the semantic projection has been successfully obtained (thereby defining the semantic model of the DSL), the syntactic level of the DSL can be obtained by a cross-model (M2M) transformation of the result of the corresponding semantic projection. The resulting syntactic DSL models are independent of each other and are defined by the end users according to the adaptation of the semantic projection to their own tasks.

Finally, the syntax models created are used by the end users of the DSL, who define a set of DSL dialects within one particular syntax model.

Thus, according to the proposed approach, the DSL is created taking into account domain knowledge and user requirements. The first fact makes it possible to organize consistent changes in the DSM and the semantic model of the DSL, while the second ensures that changes can be made to the DSL syntax without having to redefine the semantic level of the DSL.

The proposed approach differs significantly from the classical approach to the construction of DSLs (Fig. 4.3), in which the transition between the different levels of the DSL structure is implemented manually and the results of the subject area analysis, recorded in the form of a DSM, are used only informally. In this case, changes at different levels of the DSL structure cannot be implemented independently of each other because changes in DSL syntax require the initial implementation of corresponding changes at the level of DSL semantics and its metamodel. As a consequence, every change in the target subject area necessitates manual redefinition of all levels of the DSL structure. A similar process is repeated when changes to the DSL are caused by end users. As a result, the output is a set of incompatible DSL dialects that cannot be mapped to each other because of differences in all levels of the DSL structure.

Compared to traditional approaches, the proposed projection approach (Fig. 4.3, bottom) for the development of DSL software for general-purpose software systems is organized strictly according to the target domain and lifecycle of the software systems.

In this case, the results of the lifecycle stages are not only captured as artifacts but are also used in the implementation of subsequent lifecycle stages. For example, the results of the domain analysis phase are captured in the form of a semantic model of the domain (represented, e.g., as an ontology), and then this model is converted into a semantic DSL model using cross-model transformations, which in this case cannot use the full semantic model of the domain, but its individual components. This makes it possible to build several semantic models for different DSLs on one semantic model of the domain. A metamodel (abstract syntax) of the DSL is then constructed using cross-model transformations on the basis of the semantic model of the DSL, on the basis of which a concrete language syntax is subsequently defined.

As cross-model conversions are bidirectional, changes in one model can be automatically transferred to other models, thereby keeping all models consistent with each other. The only step in which user input is required remains the step of defining the specific language syntax. However, even this step is partly automated, as the user uses the DSL metamodel objects, defining only a set of commands to work with them through the DSL evolution human-machine interface built into the system.

As a result, we can define several DSL syntactic dialects within one particular DSL semantic model, which will be consistent and between which users can mutually navigate without redefining the DSL semantic models.

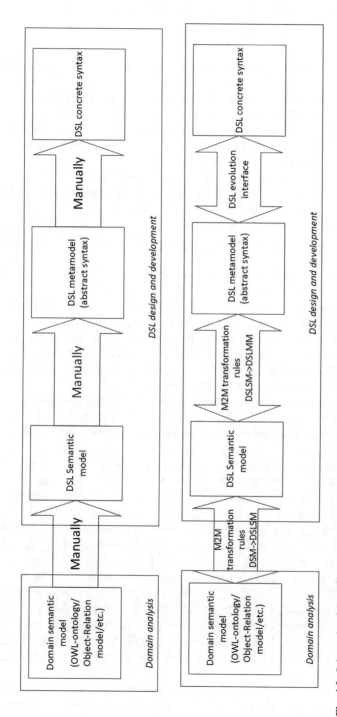

Fig. 4.3 Schematic of the differences between the traditional (top) and projection (bottom) approaches to DSL development

4.2   Representation of the DSL Evolution Under the Proposed Approach

In the previous section, we presented a description of the projection approach for DSL construction. However, as was shown in Chap. 1, along with the process of building the DSL, there is the important issue of implementing the evolution of the DSL in accordance with changes in the subject domain and user competencies.

For a complete description of the proposed approach, it is necessary to transfer it to DSL evolution procedures by describing the possible implementation of DSL evolution using the proposed projection mechanisms.

Extending the definition of a model mentioned earlier in Sect. 2.2, it can be argued that, from a formal point of view, the structure of each model is a combination of (E, R) where $E = \{e_i, \ i = 1, N\}$ is the set of some entities (each entity is a set of its attributes $e_i = \{attr_{i_1}, attr_{i_2}, \ldots, attr_{i_M}\}$, $M \in \mathbb{N}, \, i = 1, N)$ of some domain and $R = \{r_{ij} = (e_i \ e_j), \ i, j = 1, N\}$—a set of relations between entities $e_i, e_j \in E$.

In this sense, the process of model evolution can be defined as any change in the structure of the model, both in the set of entities and in the relationships between them. In the first case, we actually change the perspective (depth of detail) of the model because we refine the set of entities that appear in it. In the case of changing the relationships between entities, the perspective remains unchanged. Based on these ideas, it seems appropriate to divide the evolution of the model into two types: vertical and horizontal. Further definitions of these types of evolution are an extension of the ideas outlined in Cleenewerck [25].

Vertical evolution refers to a change in the level of conceptualization (perspective) of the model. In this type of evolution, new entities are added to the model, or existing entities are removed (with a consequent change in the set of relationships—since in a DSM, an entity cannot be "hanging" (not linked to other entities)). From a formal point of view, vertical evolution can be defined as follows: $(E^1, \ R^1)$ is the result of a vertical evolution of a model $(E, \ R)$ if $|E| \neq |E^1|$ and $|R| \neq |R^1|$. By denoting by F_v the procedure of vertical evolution, we can rewrite the above definition as follows: $F_v((E, \ R)) = (E^1, \ R^1) \implies \{|E| \neq |E^1| \uparrow R| \neq |R^1|\}$.

Given that in our case this formalism is used not only at the level of the domain model but also at the level of the DSL model, we can interpret this definition as follows. Vertical evolution of the domain model is equivalent to changes in the object level of the DSL (metamodel): some objects will be added to the metamodel, and some will be removed from it (with corresponding consequent changes in the syntax level). As a consequence and taking into account the model-oriented definition of DSL given in the previous section, it can be argued that the procedure of vertical evolution F_v is universal (since it is applicable to any model in general) and can be applied to organize a consistent vertical evolution of the DSM and DSL metamodel.

Horizontal evolution of a model, unlike vertical evolution, preserves the level of conceptualization of the model, but changes the attribute sets for some entities and/or the set of relationships between entities. From a formal point of view, horizontal evolution can be defined as follows: (E^1, R^1) is the result of the horizontal evolution of the model (E, R) if $|E| = |E^1|$ and $\exists\, e_i \in E,\ e_i^1 \in E^1$: $Attr_i \cap Attr_i^1 = Attr_i \bigwedge |Attr_i| \neq |Attr_i^1|$ and $\exists\, r_i \in R,\ r_j \in R^1 : r_i \notin R^1 \vee r_j \notin R$. By denoting by F_h the horizontal evolution procedure, we can rewrite the above definition as follows: $F_h\,((E, R)) = (E^1, R^1) \Longrightarrow \{|E| = |E^1| \exists\, e_i \in E,\ e_i^1 \in E^1 : Attr_i \cap Attr_i^1 = Attr_i \bigwedge |Attr_i| \neq |Attr_i^1| \exists\, r_i \in R,\ r_j \in R^1 : r_i \notin R^1 \vee r_j \notin R\}$.

Given that in our case this formalism is used not only at the level of the domain model but also at the level of the DSL model, it is possible to interpret this definition as follows. The horizontal evolution of the domain model is equivalent to the preservation of the object level of the DSL (metamodel) at the level of entities (objects) with changes in the set of their attributes and/or relations between them (some attributes/relationships will be added to the metamodel, and some will be removed from it (with corresponding consequent changes at the syntax level)). As a consequence, and taking into account the model-oriented definition of a DSL given in the previous section, it can be argued that the procedure of horizontal evolution F_h, as well as the procedure of vertical evolution F_v, is universal (since it is applicable to any model in general) and can be applied to organize coordinated horizontal evolution of the DSM and DSL metamodel.

Thus, using the model-oriented formalization of a DSL and DSM, we can argue that it is possible to organize the coherent evolution of all levels of a DSL and DSM by implementing vertical and horizontal evolution procedures, which are universal because they are described in terms of a common model definition.

In order to address the important question of formalizing the evolutionary procedures defined above, it is necessary to decompose these procedures down to the level of individual actions.

In the case of vertical evolution, we are actually changing the set of model entities and the relationships between them, so the necessary rules (transformations) here are:

- Creating (adding) an entity
- Entity removal
- The creation (addition) of an entity-to-entity relationship
- Removal of the relationship between entities

In the case of horizontal evolution, the perspective remains unchanged, and all changes occur only at the level of attributes of entities and/or links between entities. As a consequence, the necessary rules (transformations) here are as follows:

- Creating (adding) an attribute
- Attribute removal
- Editing the attribute
- The creation (addition) of an entity-to-entity relationship
- Removal of the relationship between entities
- Editing the relationship between entities

Given that any editing operation can be reduced to the sequential application of operations to delete and then add the corresponding entity, the rules for editing attributes and relationships between entities can be removed from this set of rules (transformations). We also do not consider in this set of rules the operation of renaming objects (entities, attributes, relationships between entities), because it is more technical and is provided by the system of implementation of model transformations, without affecting the level of formalization in any way.

Taking all of the above into account, the following set of rules is sufficient to implement any type of evolution:

- Creating (adding) an entity
- Entity removal
- The creation (addition) of an entity-to-entity relationship
- Removal of the relationship between entities
- Creating (adding) an attribute
- Attribute removal

It is important to note that this set of rules (transformations) is universal and can be applied to implement any type of evolution of any models. Consequently, it is also applicable to the implementation of a coherent evolution of DSM and models of all DSL levels.

Then, it can be argued that the operations of evolution can be formalized as follows:

$$F_v = f(Rule_{CE}, Rule_{DE}, Rule_{CR}, Rule_{DR}) \qquad (4.1)$$

$$F_h = g(Rule_{CA}, Rule_{DA}, Rule_{CR}, Rule_{DR}) \qquad (4.2)$$

where f and g are some functions (sequences of transformations) formalizing the cross-model transformations; $Rule_{CE}$ and $Rule_{DE}$, rules (cross-model transformations) for adding and removing model entities, respectively; $Rule_{CR}$ and $Rule_{DR}$, rules (cross-model transformations) for adding and removing relationships between model entities, respectively; and $Rule_{CA}$ and $Rule_{DA}$, rules (cross-model transformations) for adding and deleting attributes of model entities, respectively.

All of the rules $Rule_{CE}$, $Rule_{DE}$, $Rule_{CR}$, $Rule_{DR}$, $Rule_{CA}$, $Rule_{DA}$ defined above do not depend on which entities/relationships/attributes are used in them. These rules are dual in nature, as they apply to a set of some model objects and also require an additional parameter specifying on which of the objects in the set the transformation is to be performed.

Denoting by (E^1, R^1) the result of applying to the initial model (E, R) of the above rules, we obtain the following generalization of their behavior. Applying the rule $Rule_{CE}(E, e_{new}) \implies E^1 = \{E \cup e_{new}\}$, $Rule_{DE}(E, e_{old}) \implies E^1 = \{E \backslash e_{old}\}$. Similar behavior is characteristic of other rules, in particular $Rule_{CR}(R, r_{new}) \implies R^1 = \{R \cup r_{new}\}$ and $Rule_{DR}(R, r_{old}) \implies R^1 = \{R \backslash r_{old}\}$. By analogy, the behavior of the rule can also be represented for changing the set of attributes of the model entities, given that $e \in E$

and $e = \{attr_1, attr_2, \ldots, attr_M\}$, $M \in \mathbb{N}$: $Rule_{CA}(e, attr_{new}) \implies e' \in E^{1'} : e' = \{attr_1, attr_2, \ldots, attr_M\} \cup attr_{new} = \{e \cup attr_{new}\}$, and $Rule_{DA}(e, attr_{old}) \implies e' \in E^{1'} : e' = \{attr_1, attr_2, \ldots, attr_M\} \backslash attr_{old} = \{e \backslash attr_{old}\}$.

Thus, it can be argued that the behavior of these rules is unambiguous and does not depend on which objects are used in their implementation. Let supplement the above rules with conditions on editable elements of the source model (E, R) as follows: $p_{CE} = \{\exists e_{new} : e_{new} \notin E\}$, $p_{DE} = \{\exists e_{old} : e_{old} \in E\}$, $p_{CR} = \{\exists r_{new} : r_{new} \notin R\}$, $p_{DR} = \{\exists r_{old} : r_{old} \in R\}$, $p_{CA} = \{\exists attr_{new} : attr_{new} \notin \{attr_1, attr_2, \ldots, attr_M\}, M \in \mathbb{N}\}$, and $p_{DA} = \{\exists attr_{old} : attr_{old} \in \{attr_1, attr_2, \ldots, attr_M\}, M \in \mathbb{N}\}$. In this case, each condition denotes an essential characteristic (property) of the original model that must be fulfilled in order to apply the corresponding rule: p_{CE} ensures that the new object added to the original model is different from all existing objects, p_{DE}—conversely, that only one of the existing objects can be removed from the original model. Similarly, conditions for adding and removing relationships are formulated (p_{CR} and p_{DR}, respectively), to add and remove attributes of model objects (p_{CA} and p_{DA}, respectively).

Additionally, we formulate a set of conditions on the target models by taking as conditions the right-hand sides of the corresponding rules defined above: $q_{CE} = \{E^1 = \{E \cup e_{new}\}\}$, $q_{DE} = \{E^1 = \{E \backslash e_{old}\}\}$, $q_{CR} = \{R^1 = \{R \cup r_{new}\}\}$, $q_{DR} = \{R^1 = \{R \backslash r_{old}\}\}$, $q_{CA} = \{e' \in E^{1'} : e' = \{attr_1, attr_2, \ldots, attr_M\} \cup attr_{new}\}$, and $q_{DA} = \{e' \in E^{1'} : e' = \{attr_1, attr_2, \ldots, attr_M\} \backslash attr_{old}\}$.

These conditions define the essential characteristics (properties) of the target model, thereby ensuring the consistency of the transformations performed and the structure of the models: q_{CE} describes the set of entities of the target model in case of adding a new entity to the original model, e_{new} is obtained by combining the set of E the set of entities of the original model and the new entity e_{new}, and q_{DE} ensures that in the case of deletion of an entity e_{old} from the set E, the set of entities of the source model is obtained as a result of the logical difference E and e_{old}. Similarly, the conditions on the set of relations (attributes of entities) of the target model are formulated in the case of adding and removing relations (attributes of entities) of the source model: q_{CR} and q_{DR} (q_{CA} and q_{DA}), respectively.

Considering that F_v and F_h are a superposition of the above cross-model transformation rules, it can also be argued that in this case, evolution procedures are the result of sequential application of different cross-model transformation rules and, hence, their application also preserves the essential characteristics of the models outlined above.

This results in a set of cross-model model transformations that is independent of the form in which the DSM and the models of all levels of the DSL are represented. As a consequence, this set of rules is reusable and can be adapted to organize the evolution of any type of DSL, as will be presented in the following sections of the chapter.

The only limitation in this case is the fact that, since the technical representation of DSM and DSL level models can be done in different notations, this rule set needs to be redefined for different notations, which imposes certain limitations on its use. However, in terms of evolution, this set of rules does not change over time and, once defined, can be applied to implement any type of evolution and development of different DSLs over the same DSM defined in a given notation and can be applied to implement DSL evolution at all its levels also without change.

4.3   Algorithmization of DSL Evolution Procedures Using Cross-Model Transformations

As was shown in the previous section, to implement a transformation procedure between a DSM and a DSL metamodel, it is sufficient to define in a declarative way a set of rules for implementing cross-model transformations, including rules: $Rule_{CE}$, $Rule_{DE}$, $Rule_{CR}$, $Rule_{DR}$, $Rule_{CA}$, $Rule_{DA}$.

To define such rules, this chapter proposes the use of the ATL transformation language [7], as it allows describing in a declarative way transformation rules from any source model to any target model, conducting the transformation at the level of metamodels. Moreover, the ATL transformation language has a simple scheme for defining transformation rules consisting of only four components: rule name, type of source model element, type of equivalent target model element, and also an optional block for defining additional actions (Fig. 4.4).

In this case, the algorithmization of the DSL evolution procedures can be defined as follows:

1. The main meta-level objects of the original model (classes, etc.) are defined.
2. The main objects of the target model meta-level are defined.
3. A correspondence is established between the source and target model meta-level objects by defining the ATL transformation rules between them.
4. The specified transformation rules are applied by means of a transformation execution environment (in our case, the Eclipse Modeling Project [29]).

```
modeltype modelTypeName;

transform ruleName (
in i : originalModel, out o : targetModel
);

mapping originalModelType::originalModelElement() :
targetModelElement
{
   actions
}
```

Fig. 4.4   Scheme for defining conversion rules in ATL

```
rule    SMPOClass2DSLClass {
from a: SMPO!SMPOClass (does not exist (select b|
                            b.isTypeOf (DSL!DSLClass)
                            and a.name = b.name))
to    b: DSL!DSLClass,
      c:DSL!Constructor
}
rule DropDeletedSMPOClassInDSLClass {
from b: DSL! DSL Class (does not exist (select a|
                            a.isTypeOf (SMPO!SMPOClass)
                            and a.name = b.name))
to    drop
do { drop c: DSL!Constructor (c.name = b.name) }
}
rule SMPOClassWithParents2DSLClassWithParents {
from a: SMPO!SMPOClass (a.parent->exists())
to    b: DSL!DSLClass (b.name = a.name),
do { b.parent.name = a.parent.name }
}
rule DropDeletedSMPOClassParentsInDSLClasses {
from b: DSL!DSLClass (
            does not exist (select a|
            a.isTypeOf (SMPO!SMPOClass)
            and a.name = b.name and a.parent.name = b.parent.name))
to    drop b.parent
do { drop c: DSL!Function!DSLObjectProperty(
                    c->getProperties()->contains(b.parent)) }
}
```

Fig. 4.5 Programmed cross-model transformations for the vertical DSL evolution

The algorithm for the vertical evolution of the model (and the transfer of corresponding changes to the DSL metamodel) is based on the application of a set of declarative rules $Rule_{CE}$, $Rule_{DE}$, $Rule_{CR}$, $Rule_{DR}$. Given that the source and target models can be defined in different notations, in this case, we will define this set of rules using ATL-based pseudocode (Fig. 4.5): *SMPOClass2DSLClass* as $Rule_{CE}$, *DropDeletedSMPOClassInDSLClass* as $Rule_{DE}$, *SAMPOClassWithParents2DSLCClassWithParents* as $Rule_{CR}$, and *DropDeletedSMPOClassParentsInD-SLClasses* as $Rule_{DR}$.

In order to organize horizontal evolution, this set of rules needs to be supplemented by rules $Rule_{CA}$, $Rule_{DA}$. In terms of ATL-based pseudocode, these rules can be represented as follows (Fig. 4.6): *OWLClassAttributes2DSLClassAttributes* as $Rule_{CA}$ and *DropDeletedOWLClassAttributesInDSLClassAttributes* as $Rule_{DE}$.

It is important to note that this rule set can be used to perform all types of DSM evolution and consistent changes to the DSL metamodel. Thus, this rule set is universal and can be reused by end users to make changes to the DSM without the risk of losing consistency with the DSL.

In order for the built solution to be fully ready for use within a specific software system, a similar set of transformation rules between metamodel and DSL syntax levels must additionally be defined.

```
rule SMPOClassAttributes2DSLClassAttributes {
from a: SMPO!SMPOClass!OWLObjectProperty (
          does not exist (select b|
                  b.isTypeOf (DSL!DSLClass!DSLObjectProperty)
              and a.name = b.name))
to    b: DSL!DSLClass!DSLObjectProperty (b.owner.name = a.owner.name),
      c: DSL!Constructor!DSLObjectProperty (b.owner.name =
c.owner.name)
}
rule DropDeletedSMPOClassAttributesInDSLClassAttributes {
from b: DSL!DSLClass!DSLObjectProperty (
          does not exist (select a|
                  a.isTypeOf (SMPO!SMPOClass!SMPOObjectProperty)
              and a.name = b.name))
to    drop
do { drop c: DSL!Constructor!DSLObjectProperty (c.name = b.name) }
}
```

Fig. 4.6 Programmed cross-model transformations for the horizontal DSL evolution

Overall Conclusion In summary, this chapter proposes a new projective approach for organizing the construction and evolution of the DSL for modeling the human-machine interfaces of general-purpose software systems and considers the formalization of the proposed approach using cross-model transformations.

The proposed projection approach is based on a unified model-oriented representation of the DSL, which allows the results of the domain analysis stage, recorded in the form of a DSM, to be used in constructing all levels of the DSL structure. At the same time, the DSL structure is developed step by step and automated, using cross-model transformations, which makes the proposed approach more flexible in comparison with the classical approach to DSL development.

It is important to note that the proposed projective approach also makes it possible to ensure the consistency of different DSL dialects built on the basis of a single DSM by identifying essential features (properties) of the transformed (source and target) models, in particular the property of equivalence between DSL abstract syntax model objects and DSL objects, establishing correspondence between them at the level of the metamodel.

However, the definition of these essential characteristics (properties) does not depend on the type of DSL to be developed, because it is formulated at the level of the DSL metamodel and can be adapted to different types of DSL evolution (whose full analysis and formalization are proposed in Sect. 3.2) by applying an appropriate set of declarative rules in ATL (described in Sect. 3.3) to implement the DSL evolution.

Chapter 5
Practical Use of the Proposed Projection Approach for Developing and Modifying a DSL in Changing Contexts

Abstract This chapter presents the practical application of the proposed projection approach to DSL development and the developed algorithms for DSL evolution procedures using cross-model transformations during the development of software systems for two domains: the University Admissions Office software system and the railway station resource allocation software system. These domains demonstrate a dynamic context in which it is necessary to be able to modify the DSL structure for modelling interfaces without completely recreating the DSL.

5.1 Arguments for the Choice of Domains to Verify the Results

In the case of the program system of the University Admission Office, the changes are caused by constant adjustments to the Admission Regulation. As a consequence, the structure of the system as a whole and, in particular, the reporting system also needs refinements and adjustments. That is why the application of the proposed projection approach, which allows synchronizing the changes in the domain model and the structure of all levels of the DSL, is appropriate for this domain.

Every year, institutions of higher education enroll applicants in different fields of study. The results of entrance examinations as well as the individual achievements of the applicants are taken into account for admission. In addition, there is a set of benefits available to applicants: winners of various Olympiads, etc. Considering the possibility of admission to several specialties, we get a significant amount of data, which should be taken into account in the work of the admissions committee. In addition, every year, based on the results of the admission campaign, changes are made to the admission rules and various reporting forms. All these changes should be reflected in the subject-oriented interface to ensure consistency of the interface with the data structure.

It is important to note, however, that depending on which higher education programs are being recruited, the structure of the data used in the Admissions Committee's work will also differ. For example, admission to master's programs may take into account the results of the portfolio, while admission to bachelor's programs may not take into account the data from the bachelor's certificates. As a consequence, the staff of the admissions committee must constantly take into account the specifics of a particular admission campaign and coordinate changes in the interface with changes in the set of selection criteria for applicants to various higher education programs.

More often, the Admissions Office uses several software products or a single software product containing various independent modules to work within the admission campaign for the respective higher education program. This significantly increases the complexity of the software product, as it requires changes not in one part of it but in several at once in case of changes in admission rules. In addition, a set of reporting forms comprising around 200 different indicators is completed each year at the end of the admission campaign. For the most part, these indicators are identical for the different forms of higher education. However, due to the fact that different data system and interfaces are used for each of the admission forms, there is a need to adapt the relevant blocks of the software system, which significantly increases the time to implement the necessary changes and their time consumption.

Under these circumstances, not only the object-relational schema of the data collected during the admission campaign but also the man-machine interfaces need to be constantly improved. Due to the large amount of data collected (about 80 linked tables for 7000 records), manual interface changes are extremely difficult and time-consuming. The introduction of automation elements into the process of adapting interfaces to changes in the object-relational schema seems appropriate. In this case, changes are only made to the table structure, and the interface corrects the changes automatically. It also saves the end users from having to involve specialists (programmers) in the process of changing the interfaces, which greatly simplifies the whole process of developing and modifying the software product.

To implement the proposed automation in accordance with the previously described approach, it is necessary to identify the minimal constructive units (MCUs) at the object-relational schema level, link them to the minimal constructive components (MCCs) at the interface level, and implement the mapping function between them, using the transformation rules described and formalized earlier in Sects. 3.2 and 3.3.

In this case, by MCU, we mean the minimum object units of a model that cannot be decomposed to the level of other, smaller MCUs.

In the case of resource allocation for a railway station, there are many heterogeneous resources that are changing in real time. As a consequence, users need to have a flexible and understandable tool that allows for quick changes in the context of the resource allocation task at hand. With rolling stock arriving at the station from different transport hubs, the use of the DSL makes sense as it ensures uniform terminology used by station dispatchers and, as a consequence, software interfaces.

5.2 Development of a Software System Based on the Projection Approach for Railway Station Resource Management

According to the main provisions of the proposed projection approach, the development of a software system for railway station resource management includes the following stages: development of the domain model (DSM construction), definition of MCU at the DSM level, definition of the DSL metamodel, definition of rules for cross-model transformations between the DSM and DSL metamodel, description of MCC interfaces of future system, implementation of future system, and DSL evolution possibilities.

5.2.1 Applying the Projection Approach: Developing a Model of the Domain

The allocation and management of resources (siding, maintenance crews, etc.) in the railway station is carried out using the automated situation analysis workstation of the Traffic Control Centre (TCC ARM) [12]. Dispatcher is responsible for the placement and removal of cars, rational use of shunting locomotives and wagons, loading and unloading fronts and mechanisms, execution of the loading plan and standards of turnover of cars, making adjustments to the work plan on receiving information about the supply of cars on the approach track, and keeping records of completed work [21].

As mentioned earlier, we will use a domain ontology as a DSM (fragments are presented in Fig. 5.1), represented in terms of UML diagram (main components of which were described in Sect. 3.3). This model contains the attributes of the main objects of the domain and methods for working with them (resources of the railway station in this case). This model contains the attributes of the main objects of the domain and methods for working with them (resources of the railway station in this case). For example, a wagon is characterized by such attributes as a unique identifier, type (freight, passenger, transportation, etc.), service priority (from "extra urgent" to "on schedule"), length (number of cars), arrival and departure time, reserve time for parking, and the number of wagons to service. To implement train maintenance, it is possible to use such methods as *createTrain()* (sets a wagon with specific attribute values), *deleteTrain()* (for example, in case of service cancellation), *allocateTrainToRailway()* and *rellocateTrainBetweenRailways()* (in order to resolve conflicts in the territorial location of trains), etc.

When assigning tracks to different rolling stock, characteristics such as track specialization (some tracks are designed to serve only certain types of trains (freight/passenger/train), availability of operations (services), availability of equipment to carry out the relevant service, etc. are taken into account [11].

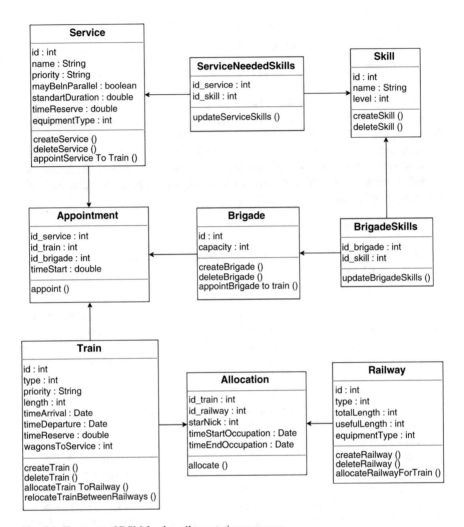

Fig. 5.1 Fragment of DSM for the railway station resources

It is also important to consider the technical characteristics of the rolling stock: length, load factor, etc. [21]. The parameters of the resource management task of a railway station are presented in more detail in Table 5.1. This set of variables is a complete list of attributes needed to solve the resource allocation problem in real time. It is not redundant and yet leaves for flexible management of the constraint satisfaction procedure during the search for an optimal solution to the problem.

Table 5.1 Parameters of the station resource management task

Parameter	Description
$1..M$	Rolling stock numbers
$1..K$	Access route numbers
L_j	Length j-th access road
l_i	Length i-rolling stock
N_i	The number of wagons to be serviced in i-th train
$Tarr_i$	Arrival time i-th rolling stock
Tsw_i	Start time i-of rolling stock
Top_i	Expected service time i-of rolling stock
W_i	Track number for i-th rolling stock
$C_{i,0}$	Initial position i-of the rolling stock on the track
$\delta_{i,t}$	Displacement value i-of the rolling stock at the time t
$Tcur$	Current time
$Tshift_{i,t}$	The time taken to shift i-of the rolling stock at a point in time t

These variables must satisfy the constraints presented in (Eq. 5.1).

$$
\begin{cases}
t \in [0; T_{\max}] \\
Tcur \in [0; T_{\max}] \\
Top_i \geq 0 \\
Tarr_i \in [0; T_{\max}], \ i = 1..M \\
Tsw_i \in [0; T_{\max}], \ i = 1..M \\
Tsw_i \geq Tarr_i, \ i = 1..M \\
1 \leq W_i \leq K, \ i = 1..M \\
0 \leq C_{i,0} \leq L_{W_i}, \ i = 1..M \\
\sum_{i: \ W_i=j} l_i \leq L_j, i = 1..M, \ j = 1..K \\
\delta_{i,t} = -\infty, \ t < Tarr_i, \ i = 1..M \\
\delta_{i,v} = 0, \ i = 1..M, \ v = Tarr_i \ and \ Tsw_i \leq v \leq Tsw_i + Top_i \\
0 \leq C_{i,0} + \sum_{t=0}^{Tcur} \delta_{i,t} \leq L_{W_i}, i = 1..M \\
0 \leq C_{i,0} + \sum_{t=0}^{Tcur} \delta_{i,t} + l_i \leq L_{W_i}, i = 1..M \\
C_{i,0} + \sum_{t=0}^{Tcur} \delta_{it} + l_i \leq C_{i+1,0} + \sum_{t=0}^{Tcur} \delta_{i+1,t}, i = 1..(M-1)
\end{cases}
\tag{5.1}
$$

The first six equations of the system (Eq. 5.1) include the constraints imposed on the time characteristics of the arriving train: the arrival and staging times, the constraint that the train service does not start until after arrival.

The remaining eight constraints in the system (Eq. 5.1) are related to the spatial and technical limitations of the rolling stock and the siding: the possible location of trains in space, their shift over time (with the length of the train not exceeding the length of the siding, including the shift), the prohibition on shifting for the serviced train, and the inability to "overlap" trains with each other (the end of the train must not coincide with the beginning of the train on the same siding).

This set of variables defines the context of the rolling stock and other resource allocation problem to be solved, and the values of these variables may vary and not be the same for different DSL scenarios for modelling the MCC of the software system.

There are two options on how to pass the required parameter values to the DSL model and then to the solver: either directly include them in the DSL description or use an existing solution that involves organizing access to databases (DBs) with the relevant information. For the purposes of this work, we use the first option, as the DSL to be created is reconfigurable, which means that its syntax (and other levels) can change over time, which can make the support and use of the database required in the second option much more difficult.

A detailed diagram of the railways resource model required for the resource allocation task is presented in Appendix C. As can be seen from this diagram, it contains all the information that may be needed in the process of solving the resource allocation problem and includes all the main characteristics of these resources, including the links between them, implemented through additional communication classes.

5.2.2   Applying the Projection Approach: Describing MCUs in DSL Models

As shown in Sect. 3.3, once a model of the domain has been defined, we can derive a metamodel of the DSL using a system of cross-model transformations. However, regardless of whether we define the transformation (operational or relational) in the form presented in Sect. 2.2, we need to know the structural units (MCUs) of the target and source model languages to establish a correspondence between them.

In this case, the DSM is represented in an ontological representation (in OWL notation), and the DSL metamodel is formalized as an object-relational model [49].

In the case of a railway station, we assume that two interlinked DSLs are appropriate: one of them is visual and is used to display the current resource allocation, while the second one (textual) is used to control the set of resources by the dispatcher and manually make corrections in the task context. Each of these DSLs requires its own description, which is used for implementation in the program.

In the case of a textual DSL MCU, the language of user commands (scripts) is described by means of regular expressions, because textual DSLs do not only involve checking the correctness of scripts but also defining the structure of commands. As a consequence, this type of DSL has little functionality and does not require a full-fledged grammar with lexical and syntactic parsers. In this case, regular expressions are created dynamically based on user-defined constructs. For example, for a command to place a train on a particular path from a particular point, a regular expression might look like this

$$(put\ train)()(\backslash d+)()(on\ railway)()(\backslash d+)(with)()(\backslash d+)$$

```
Domainmodel:
    (elements+=AbstractElement)*;

PackageDeclaration:
    'package' name=QualifiedName '{'
        (elements+=AbstractElement)*
    '}';

AbstractElement:
    PackageDeclaration | Type | Import;

QualifiedName:
    ID ('.' ID)*;

Import:
    'import'
importedNamespace=QualifiedNameWithWildcard;

QualifiedNameWithWildcard:
    QualifiedName '.*'?

Type:
    DataType | Entity;

DataType:
    'datatype' name=ID;
```

Fig. 5.2 Fragment of the BN-grammar

However, in order to create a set of commands for managing DSL objects, a set of commands for creating (modifying) DSL objects must also be provided to the user. This set of commands can be defined using a context-free grammar, described in Becus-Naur form as follows (Fig. 5.2).

It is important to note that this grammar is not created from scratch but is constructed in automated mode on the basis of the DSL metamodel. In our case, since DSL development is done with Eclipse plug-ins, it is reasonable to present the DSL metamodel as an Ecore model [63], which supports all the basic blocks of object-oriented representation and for which there is an automatic translator in the form of a grammar. A complete set of textual DSL commands is presented in Appendix D.

5.2.3   Applying the Projection Approach: Describing Cross-Model Transformations Between DSM and DSL Metamodels

Once the MCU at the level of the DSL metamodel have been identified, cross-model transformations between the DSM and the DSL metamodel can be defined.

This requires applying the set of rules described in Sect. 3.3, adapting them to transform the ontology model into a DSL metamodel in accordance with the notations of the DSM representation and the DSL metamodel. The resulting set of rules in terms of the ATL transformation language is presented in Appendix C.

In order to define transformation rules between metamodel and DSL syntax levels, it is necessary, by analogy with the allocation of MCUs at the metamodel level, to allocate MCUs at the DSL syntax level, in our case also defining the architecture of the proposed systems.

5.2.4   Applying the Projection Approach: Describing the MCC in the Architecture of the Proposed System

As indicated in the previous sections, in the case of a railway station, we consider two types of DSLs: textual and visual (graphical). The textual DSL was discussed in Sect. 5.2.2, so in this section, we will take a closer look at the main components of the visual DSL.

In this case, we consider the graphical user interface as a visual DSL, which can be regarded as a special kind of DSL (as shown in Sect. 2.3). The main window of the interface displays a block for specifying text DSL scenarios (together with a block with user accessible commands of this DSL), as well as a block for schematic visualization of the current location of rolling stock on the siding tracks (Fig. 5.3).

The block of user-accessible commands contains not only the names of the relevant commands but also their syntax. Technically, this list of commands is found using the Java reflection API, and their structure is deserialized.

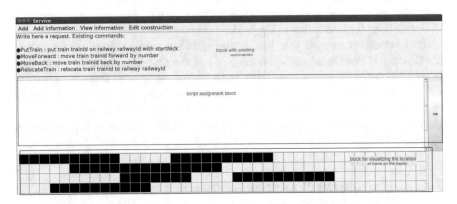

Fig. 5.3 Service main window

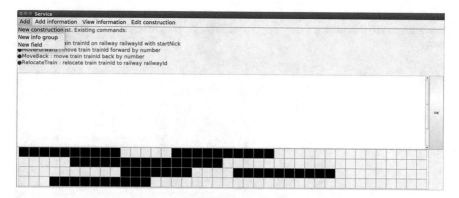

Fig. 5.4 Interface to the DSL component add-on box

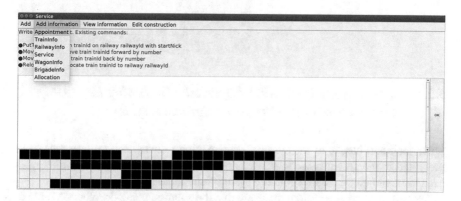

Fig. 5.5 Information group selection box interface

The menu items include Add, Add information, View information, and Edit construction. In the Add menu (Fig. 5.4), the user has the functionality to add a new language construction, a new info group, and a new field. These interface components, as well as the edit construction command, are related to the evolution of the DSL and will be discussed later.

The Add information menu item contains information groups for selection (Fig. 5.5). When selecting an information group, a window opens, containing its corresponding fields, which the user can fill in (Fig. 5.6).

We do not dwell here on the implementation of the individual components of the visual DSL as they are supportive of the textual DSL constructs, whose MCU have been described in the previous sections.

Fig. 5.6 Interface for adding information to an information group

5.2.5 Applying the Projection Approach: Designing the Architecture of the Proposed Software System

Since the main blocks of the system for managing railway station resources were presented in the previous section, in this section, we will only list the technologies used to implement the corresponding system functionality.

We use JastAdd as a system to ensure that the solution being developed is able to evolve [53], a meta-compiler system that allows us to implement compiler behavior based on attribute grammars. Apart from the fact that in JastAdd one can create standard functions to deal with abstract grammars, this system provides the ability to implement additional logic for analysis using the mechanism of attribute grammars. However, JastAdd does not provide a model focused on language description reuse. This limitation is due to the fact that in JastAdd, each declared behavior rewrites previously created system artefacts, giving the possibility to add or slow down the compilation phase.

In order to eliminate the limitations of JastAdd, we also use the extensible compiler Polyglot [84], which supports creating compilers for languages similar to Java. Based on an extensible parser generator, Polyglot allows language syntax extensions to be expressed as changes to the grammar in Java.

Finally, given the use of not only visual but also textual DSL, our system uses a plug-in for Eclipse Xtext [113]. The Xtext generator uses Eclipse's modelling process technology, and the code is generated based on the DSL metamodel. The software framework is not focused on creating a compiler but on converting one model (including text) to another.

Finally, we use ANTLR to define the grammar of the textual DSL itself [4], since Xtext not only allows us to generate the ANTLR grammar from the DSL metamodel but also automatically allows us to generate lexical and syntactic parsers for the constructed grammar together with the Java classes that store it and the editor with all the features of the environment (including code generation) [113].

5.2.6 Design and Implementation of the DSL Evolution Module

Consider the MCC blocks created to implement the evolution of the DSL. As in the case of the DSL evolution for the Admission Board software system, the DSL for railway station resource management must also support all evolution scenarios, both vertical and horizontal (similar to those highlighted in the previous section). For this purpose, the following components have been developed in the DSL evolution module.

Editing Existing Commands and Adding New Ones
If a new command is created, the user must enter its name in the window (Fig. 5.7).

Once the command name is set, a new window will appear in which the user specifies all the required blocks of the command to be created (Fig. 5.8). This

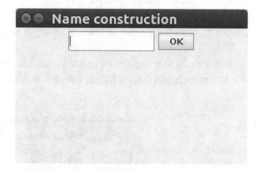

Fig. 5.7 Interface for defining the DSL construction name

Fig. 5.8 Interface for creating (editing) the DSL command

window is identical for the case of editing an existing command, so we merge these DSL evolution scenarios in this block.

To create a textual DSL design (Fig. 5.8), the user has to specify the syntax of the command itself (Construction), its corresponding constraints (Corresponding constraints), and the set of actions to be performed after launching the command. To specify the constructions, both existing class fields and user-defined variables of different domains (e.g., number or date) can be used. In the restriction specification section, the user can use all fields defined within the command syntax as well as additional keywords and symbols (e.g., "domain," "all," ","). Since there can be more than one constraint, the interface provides the ability to add new panels to which the constraints will be placed (Add line button).

Creation of Information Groups
In addition to creating/editing DSL constructions, it is also possible to create new information groups (Fig. 5.9). Similar to adding a new command, the user must first specify the name of the group to be created and whether it is a repository (an information group that combines information on the key fields of several other information groups). The user must then specify the required fields of the information group (Add field) by defining their names and type (domain).

Editing Information Groups
In addition to creating new information groups, the user can also add fields to existing groups. To do so, he needs to select an existing information group in the relevant interface component and define the necessary changes to it (e.g., add a new field) (Fig. 5.10).

The functionality discussed in this section covers all possible evolution scenarios for textual DSL, since it supports not only vertical evolution when the composition

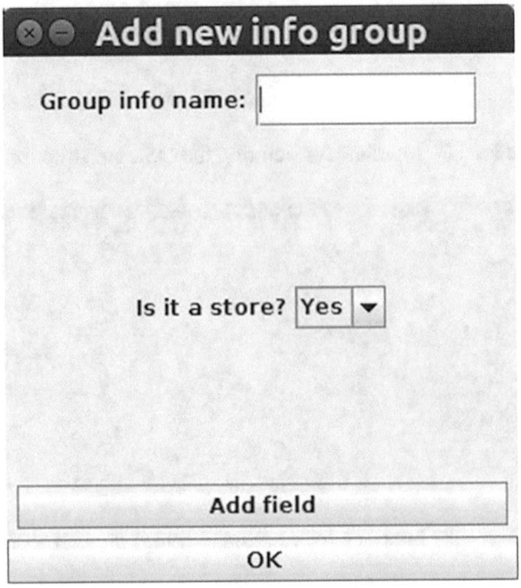

Fig. 5.9 Information group creation interface

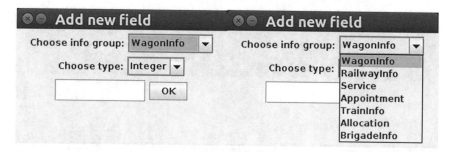

Fig. 5.10 Interface for adding a field to an information group

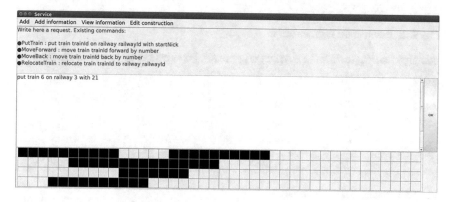

Fig. 5.11 PutTrain scenario

of an information group changes and new DSL objects are added but also horizontal evolution, which involves changing the composition of textual DSL commands.

5.2.7   Analysis of the Effectiveness of the Proposed Solution

In order to assess the effectiveness of the constructed DSL for the management of railway station resources, consider its use in several scenarios.

Suppose we have four sidings on which five trains are currently placed. A new rolling stock (№6) arrives at the station, which we want to place on track №3 from starting point 21.

To execute this script, we can use the appropriate textual DSL command by typing it into the appropriate interface window (Fig. 5.11).

From a technical point of view, the following actions will take place within the system during the execution of this scenario. First, the regular expression parser checks the correctness of the user-entered DSL construct by comparing it with the *PutTrainRule* rule defined in the system for the *put train* command. If the entered construction is correct, the data from it is augmented with constraints read from the

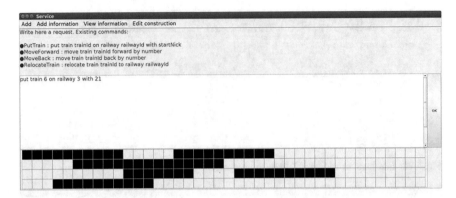

Fig. 5.12 Result of the PutTrain script

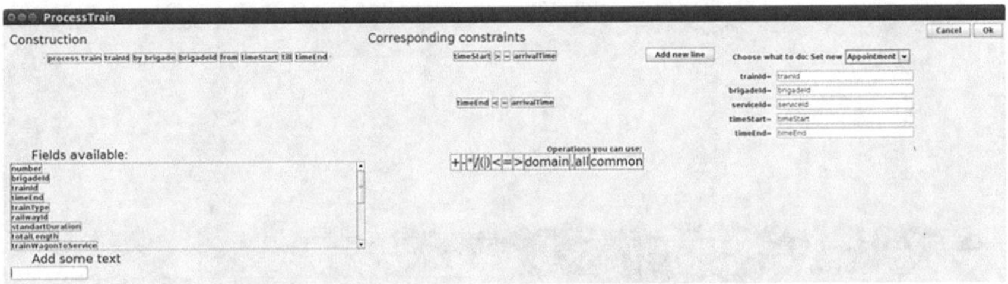

Fig. 5.13 Adding a new command

PutTrainRule rule by the Java reflection, and a constraint table is generated for the solver. Finally, the constraint table is fed to the solver, which tries to find a solution (allocation of trains between tracks) given the refined problem context. In this case, the solution is found, so it is fixed and displayed on the corresponding panel of the visual DSL (interface), as shown in Fig. 5.12.

Similarly, the user can create other scripts in the textual DSL using the relevant interface components (visual DSL).

In addition to executing existing DSL scripts, the user can also make changes to the command structure of the textual DSL using the system components listed in the previous sections.

Suppose that the user needs to define a new command in the text DSL as follows: *process train trainId by brigade brigadeId from timeStart till timeEnd* (Fig. 5.13).

As described above, to create a command, the user first sets its name and then the syntax and corresponding constraints (with a set of actions). For this purpose, the sections of the respective interface component Construction and Corresponding constraints are used.

In this case, we define the command in the form given above, supplemented by constraints of the form: timeStart >= arrivalTime and timeEnd <= arrivalTime (Fig. 5.13).

If all required fields are filled in successfully, the command will be created and immediately available to the end users. For example, we can run a scenario using the created command and redirect the rolling stock №1 to the approach track №1 (Fig. 5.14).

As can be seen, in this case, the new command is successfully recognized by the system and results in the successful execution of the user-defined script (Fig. 5.15).

In addition to adding new commands, the user can also modify existing ones. For example, replace the syntax of the *process train* command just created with the following: *process train trainId by brigade brigadeId between startTime and endTime*. This uses the same interface as the one used to create the new DSL command. After making all necessary changes in the command's syntax, we get the output of the working language construct (Fig. 5.16).

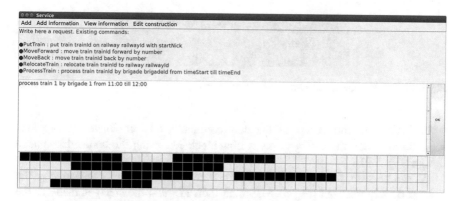

Fig. 5.14   Applying the ProcessTrain command

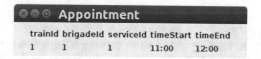

Fig. 5.15   Result of the ProcessTrian command

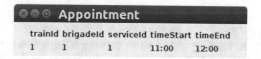

Fig. 5.16   Changing the syntax of the ProcessTrain command

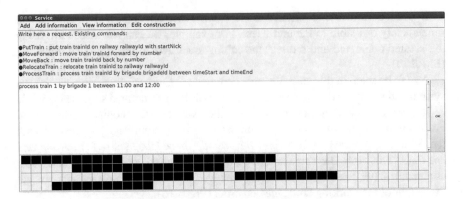

Fig. 5.17 Updated scenario for using the ProcessTrain command

trainId	brigadeId	serviceId	timeStart	timeEnd
1	1	1	11:00	12:00

Fig. 5.18 Result of the updated ProcessTrain command

To verify the correctness of the new command, let's complete the previous scenario to assign the siding to the rolling stock №1 using the updated language design (Fig. 5.17).

As can be seen, the result of the modified command is exactly the same as the one previously received (Fig. 5.18), which indicates that the changes made to the DSL did not affect its performance in any way, but was successfully applied to all levels of the DSL.

After considering the scenario of horizontal evolution of the DSL, let us consider an example of implementing a more complex vertical evolution by creating a new information group and adding a field to an existing information group. This change is more complex because it affects not only the syntax of the DSL but also the metamodel level and even the DSM.

Add a new information group to the system, *TrainInfo*. As shown earlier in Sect. 5.2.6, this requires defining the name of the new group, its fields, and whether it is a repository (Fig. 5.19).

Once the new group has been successfully created, let's add another field to it—*arrivalTime* (Fig. 5.20). This will check both the functionality of creating a new information group and editing an existing one.

To check if the operations we performed were successful, we should try to add information on the created information group (create an instance of the corresponding object class) using the corresponding interface component (Fig. 5.21). As we can see, a new information group is available for us to fill with information.

Additionally, we can check that the created information group (and all its attribute fields) is also available to us in the textword construction editor. As can

Fig. 5.19 Creating a
TrainInfo info group

Fig. 5.20 Adding a field to
the TrainInfo info group

be seen, all fields of the created information group (including the new *arrivalTime*
field) are available to the user (Fig. 5.22); hence, vertical evolution is successfully
implemented and at all levels of the DSL (both at the syntax level—we can use
created fields in language commands) and at the level of metamodel and DSM,
since the created object (information group) is correctly recognized by the system.

Thus, we can see that the service built on the basis of different types of DSLs
fully satisfies the requirement to implement a consistent and automated evolution of
the DSL. Both horizontal evolution and vertical evolution are available to the user. It
is not necessary to recreate the whole system and the DSL, because all changes are
coordinated in real time. This advantage and flexibility of the system are achieved by
implementing the evolution procedures described earlier in Sect. 3.2, implemented
in the system through the ATL transformation rules of Sect. 5.2.3.

In this case, the efficiency of the system is also ensured by the ability to modify
it without changing the source code. In this case, this advantage is even more

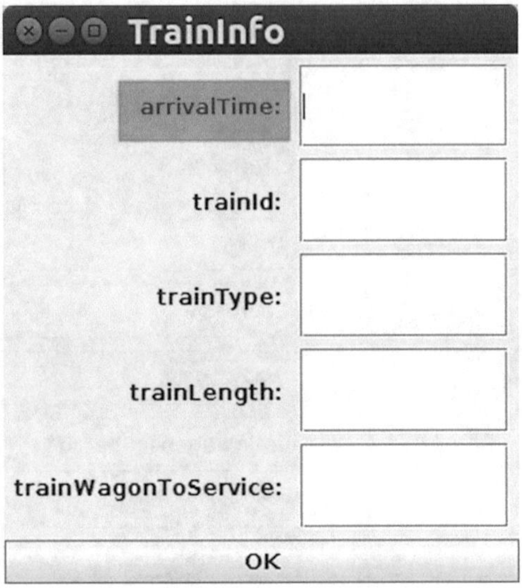

Fig. 5.21 Adding information to TrainInfo with field added

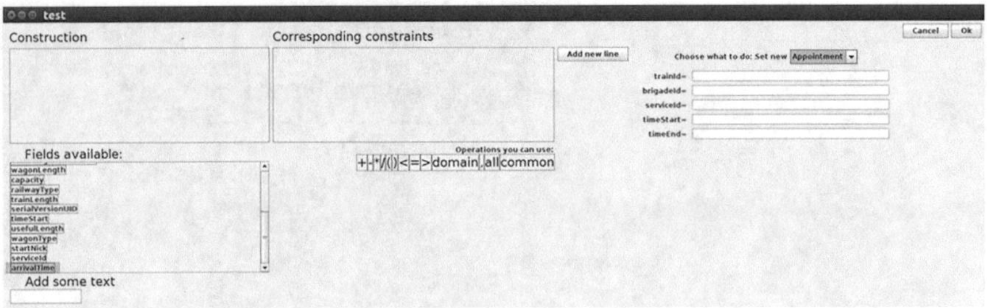

Fig. 5.22 Creating a new design with an added field

noticeable, since the changes made to the system affect not only the language syntax but also the metamodel of the DSL. As a consequence, the number of needed source code corrections would have doubled without application of the suggested approach.

So, for example, in this case, when creating a new information group without the considered approach, the user would have to change the grammar of the DSL metamodel (describing both the entity as a whole and all its attributes together with domains), parser fragments to recognize appropriate commands associated with the created entity, and constraint fragments associated with the created entity—for the solver.

Finally, syntactic constructions at the level of the specific DSL syntax. In total, these changes (in the example above) would amount to about 2000 lines of source code in all system components. In the proposed system, on the other hand, thanks to a set of rules implemented to implement a consistent evolution of the DSM and all DSL levels, these changes are made automatically, and the user does not need to change the source code of the various system components.

Furthermore, the user may not generally have in-depth knowledge of language grammars and programming, as all changes are formulated in an understandable (domain-aligned) way through the system interface and applied (translated) to all levels of the DSL automatically.

As a consequence, the potential for error in making changes to the application source code is greatly reduced, which is also an advantage of the proposed system and approach as a whole.

Evaluating the constructed solution against the currently used SW-system for the allocation of trains, the following estimate of the effectiveness of the constructed solution in terms of time is obtained (Tables 5.2 and 5.3).

In this case, it can be seen that when resources are allocated to a maximum of 50 trains, the system built is faster than the existing system. This advantage is due to the fact that DSL scenarios are formulated and processed faster than commands in the existing SW-system, which uses built-in command-to-machine converters. In the case of a DSL, in fact, script processing leads directly to constructing the required objects and passing them to the solver for finding a solution.

However, in the case of more trains (more than 50), it takes longer for the system to allocate resources than the existing system. This suggests that the built system has limitations on the scale of application—for single stations, where the flow of trains does not exceed 50 trains in 3 hours, the system is effective. On a larger scale, however, it is necessary to refine the system in terms of optimizing the solution search algorithms.

Table 5.2 Average time of distribution of railway station resources in current SW-system (unit of change: seconds)

| Time step (hour) | Number of trains (pcs.) | | | |
№	10	25	50	100
1	1,963718	4,662647	7,29648	28,61768
2	10,38311	16,2325	23,47861	160,2721
3	20,93453	60,60084	174,3898	280,191

Table 5.3 Average distribution time of railway station resources in the developed system (unit of change: seconds)

| Time step (hour) | Number of trains (pcs.) | | | |
№	10	25	50	100
1	1,785198373	3,330461987	6,080400409	31,84555657
2	7,416509162	12,48653808	16,77043755	166,1984714
3	17,445438005	35,64755483	116,2598977	288,136414

5.3   Development of a Software System Based on the Projection Approach for the University Admissions Office

5.3.1   Applying the Projection Approach: Developing a Model of the Domain

Before starting to develop a system with an Admission Office workstation, a complete semantic model of the domain must be built. In our case, since the model will later be used as the basis for the development of the semantic model and the metamodel of the DSL, the main aspects are the attributive aspects required in defining the object level (metamodel) of the DSL.

A detailed scheme of the domain model contains all the information that may be needed during the Admissions Committee process and includes all the main characteristics and data that an Applicant needs to provide when applying to the Admissions Committee.

The central entity of the schema is the Entrant entity, which includes the entire set of information characterizing the Applicant: identifier (personal file number), full name, gender, date of birth, place of birth, etc. In addition to the main entity, there are auxiliary, characterizing categories of information also related to the Applicant and the process of his admission to the university, namely, Entrance Test, Passport Data, Education, Contact Data, Special Entry Rights (including Entry Without Entrance Test, Entry for 100 Points in a Subject, Preferred Entry Right), Individual Achievement, Competitive Groups, etc. It is important to note that each of these entities has an identical set of attributes, including an identifier, name of the information category, and code in the Federal Information System (FIS). In some cases, the attribute set is supplemented with attributes specific to each category of information: for example, the Entrance Test has an additional minimum score for the subject, and the Individual Achievement has a maximum score for the corresponding achievement of the entrant. However, the basic attributes are always present and constitute one of the MCU variants of this model.

The relationship between the auxiliary entities and the main entity (Applicant) is organized through appropriate relational relationships. These relationships are implemented by means of relationship objects of the corresponding object-relational model. Each such object displays the key attributes of the entities whose relationship is fixed by the corresponding object, as well as additional attributes of the relationship. So, for example, the Entrant to Entrance Test relationship object captures the identifiers of the entrant and the entrance test, as well as the entrant's actual score on this test (to be able to further check the constraint specified in the attribute with the minimum score on the entrance test). A similar relationship links other auxiliary entities with the main Entrant entity.

Based on the projection approach outlined in the previous sections of this chapter, it can be argued that the model built is the basis for further construction of the

DSL metamodel. In our case, the DSL is a graphical interface; hence, we need to identify the MCUs at the domain model level and build correspondences for them at the interface level, creating blanks for the corresponding MCUs and defining the correspondence function between them. To do this, we first need to identify the MCU of the object-relational model used in our case to represent knowledge about the domain.

5.3.2 Applying the Projection Approach: Describing MCUs in DSL Models

In this case, the DSM is represented in an ontological representation (in OWL notation), and the OWL metamodel is formalized in an object-oriented representation in KM3 notation. The OWL ontological DSM in this case contains 70 classes with more than 110 relations. It is important to note that the model contains not only "pure" classes that are equivalent to domain entities but also communication classes that make it easier to work with relationships between entities.

In the case of a model, the MCU is the part of the structure that does not change during the evolution of the model, both vertically and horizontally.

In our case, we are considering the MCU at the metamodel level. This is due to the fact that we cannot consider the model objects themselves as the MCU, since the set of objects, as well as their attributes and relations between them, may change over time.

Moreover, by asserting the immutability of model objects, we restrict the user to the possible transformations of the model, which also contradicts the definition of dynamic context, which implies the modification of all components of the system.

Based on these assumptions, in the case of the object-relational model, we also distinguish the MCU at the metamodel level, i.e., the structure of the objects themselves.

From a formal point of view, an object-relational model is constructed as follows (in this definition, we follow [14] and [40]).

Let $A_1, \ldots, A_n$ be attributes. Each attribute A_i ($i = 1, \ldots, n$) corresponds to a valid set of values D_i ($i = 1, \ldots, n$), which the attribute can take A_i and which is called the domain of the corresponding attribute. By definition, domains are non-empty finite or countable sets. In terms of object-relational theory, this definition is supplemented by the fact that the domain is regarded as the set of values of one (and simple) data type. Scheme of the relation $R\{A_1, \ldots, A_n\}$ is a finite set of attributes $\{A_1, \ldots, A_n\}$, with the attribute A_i ($i = 1, \ldots, n$) taking a value from the set D_i ($i = 1, \ldots, n$) where n is the articulation of the relation.

Based on this definition, it can be argued that, at the meta-level, an object-relational model is characterized by a set of attributes of appropriate types. While the set of attributes may change over time, the set of domains is a finite set and does not change over time in terms of all possible schema variants.

As a consequence, all possible domains constitute the set of MCUs of the object-relational model. Given that only an elementary data type can be a domain, we can obtain the following set of MCUs for the object-relational model:

- int/integer/Num(*) is an integer,
- float/double is a floating point number,
- char(*)/varchar(*)/varchar2(*)/text—string of limited or unlimited length,
- bool/boolean/bit is a logical variable,
- Date—date,
- Time is time,
- et al.

It is then necessary to define a corresponding DSL-level MCC for each corresponding MCU of the object-relational model to organise cross-model transformations between them.

It is also possible to define as an MCU a column of values as a whole, namely, an MCU for a finite set of values of the same type. This is also useful from the point of view that the column values should not only be displayed on the screen as single values but also as a set of alternatives, e.g., as a drop-down list.

5.3.3   Applying the Projection Approach: Describing Cross-Model Transformations Between DSM and DSL Metamodels

In this case, the description of cross-model transformations is done similarly to the rules described for the railway station domain (Sect. 5.2.3).

The rule set in this case is modified by replacing the left-hand parts of the rules described in Sect. 3.3 with the corresponding MCUs highlighted in the previous section.

5.3.4   Applying the Projection Approach: Describing the MCC in the Architecture of the Proposed System

Once the MCUs at the object-relational model level have been defined, it is necessary to define their equivalents at the interface level (DSL). To do this, we define the corresponding graphical equivalent for each data type in the object-relational model. In doing so, consider that in terms of the object-relational model, not only the domain is important but also the name of the column that contains the values of that domain. This assumption is necessary to distinguish between columns with the same domain but different names.

Fig. 5.23 Schematic definition of the MCC structure of the DSL

Thus, we obtain that the MCC at the DSL level must display a pair of values (A, D) where A is the name of the corresponding column and D its domain. Graphically, this might look like splitting the domain into two parts (Fig. 5.23). Here A' is responsible for displaying the name of the corresponding MCU of the object-relational model, and D' provides for controlling the value of a corresponding column A and is defined depending on the domain D.

Given that programming languages have patterns for specifying values of relevant types, it is possible to define the following MCCs at interface level to correspond to the MCU of the object-relational model (Table 5.4).

Table 5.4 Correspondence between MCUs of the object-relational model and DSL MCCs

The MCU of the object-relational model	DSL MCC
int / integer / Num(*)	NameOfElement [ ]
float / double	NameOfElement [ ]
char(*) / varchar(*) / varchar2(*) / text	NameOfElement [ ]
bool / boolean / bit	☐ nameOfElement
Date	nameOfElement [🔲]
Time	NameOfElement [▾] [▾]
Set of values of one domain (column)	NameOfElement [▾]
Scheme	No columns in table

```
...
foreach column_invariant do
  foreach interface_invariant do
    if mapping_function(column_invariant) == interface_invariant then
      add interface_invariant onto GUI
...
```

Fig. 5.24 Pseudocode of the matching function between MCU and MCC

As can be seen, the resulting correspondence is in full accordance with the previously highlighted structure of the MCC: Thus, the left side of the MCC contains the field *nameOfElement*, which contains the name of the corresponding column of the object-relational model. On the right-hand side, there is a control element for the value of the corresponding column, defined by means of the interface pattern for the corresponding data type (e.g., dateChooser in case of date, text in case of textField, etc.).

We have also additionally defined the MCC for the schema as a whole, since the correspondence for an object-relational model table is also the area containing the components of that table.

Once the MCU at the object-relational model level and the MCC at the interface level have been constructed, a correspondence function between them must be defined. This function is the equivalent of the cross-model transformation rules defined earlier in Sect. 3.3.

However, since in our case the interface is created through source code, the transformation is not in the form of a rule but in the form of a function that establishes the correspondence between the object-relational model's MCU and the interface's MCC (in terms of source code). In the form of pseudocode, this function can be described as follows (Fig. 5.24).

As you can see, this function analyzes all object-relational model MCUs in a loop and finds a match in the DSL MCC set by comparing the domain of the object-relational model MCU with the name of the corresponding DSL MCC. If it matches, the MCC is added to the form and displayed on the interface. The software implementation of this function will be described below.

5.3.5   Applying the Projection Approach: Designing the Architecture of the Proposed Software System

When designing the system, in addition to the previously stated ideas of separating the MCU and MCC, the following assumptions must also be introduced.

The first of these is that we will follow the rule that each tab will be linked to one relationship table when constructing the DSL. Considering that in the structure of the object-relational model in our case each relationship table is linked to one main table and several auxiliary tables, it turns out that any tab will refer to one record of the main table and several auxiliary tables. However, since from the auxiliary

Fig. 5.25 MCC functional GUI interface

tables we are only interested in the column values themselves with the name of the corresponding category of information, in fact, in the case of a DSL, it will be an additional MCC of the corresponding set of values of the same type.

The second assumption relates to the fact that we believe that the full functionality of the object-oriented model is implemented through the system, namely, creating new records, editing existing records, and deleting them. As a consequence, an additional functional MCC can be provided at the interface level to display the relevant functionality. Since the interface is controlled through buttons, the following MCC is additionally introduced (Fig. 5.25).

Finally, since in our case the interface is constructed as a superposition of multiple MCCs, it is possible to introduce an object MCC of the interface tab consisting of two parts: one showing the MCC corresponding to the structure of the communication table linked to the interface tab and the other showing the MCCs providing the interaction with the corresponding table.

The structure of the main interface itself is based on the main functionality of the system, which includes the following aspects (a schematic of each individual tab is presented in the Appendix).

Basic Information

When you select a specific applicant in the table, the "Basic Information" section will become available on the right side of the window, where data with basic information on the selected applicant will be available. By clicking on the "Edit" button, the user is able to adjust the data for this applicant. By clicking on the "Save" button, the system checks that the information is correct. If all the information is correct, the system writes the information to the applicants' database by calling the stored SQL-procedure. Otherwise, the system generates a pop-up window (displayed on the screen) with an error message and highlights the data that do not meet the conditions of verification in red. The user is then prompted to make the necessary changes to the data entry panel, after which the verification process is repeated again. If another entrant is selected, the information entered will be lost if it has not been saved, and the panel will exit edit mode.

Passport Details

Selecting the Passport tab at the bottom of the main window opens the education data viewer for the selected applicant. By clicking on the "Edit" button, the user is able to adjust the data for this applicant. By pressing the "Save" button, the system checks if the information is correct. If all the information is correct, the system writes the information to the applicants' database by calling the stored SQL-procedure. Otherwise, the system generates a pop-up window (displayed on the screen) with an error message and highlights the data that do not meet the conditions of verification in red. The user is then prompted to make the necessary changes to the data entry panel, after which the verification process is repeated again. If another entrant is selected, the information entered will be lost if it has not been saved, and the panel will exit edit mode.

Education

Selecting the Education tab at the bottom of the main window opens the education data viewer for the selected applicant. By clicking on the "Edit" button, the user is able to adjust the data for this applicant. By pressing the "Save" button, the system checks if the information is correct. If all the information is correct, the system writes the information to the applicants' database by calling the stored SQL-procedure. Otherwise, the system generates a pop-up window (displayed on the screen) with an error message and highlights the data that do not meet the conditions of verification in red. The user is then prompted to make the necessary changes to the data entry panel, after which the verification process is repeated again. If another entrant is selected, the information entered will be lost if it has not been saved, and the panel will exit edit mode.

Address and Contacts

Selecting the "Address & Contacts" tab at the bottom of the main window opens a pane to view the address and contact data for the selected applicant. By clicking on the "Edit" button, the user is able to adjust the data for this applicant. By clicking "Save," the system checks that the information is correct. If all the information is correct, the system writes the information to the applicants' database by calling the stored SQL-procedure. Otherwise, the system generates a pop-up window (displayed on the screen) with an error message and highlights the data that do not meet the conditions of verification in red. The user is then prompted to make the necessary changes to the data entry panel, after which the verification process is repeated again. If another entrant is selected, the information entered will be lost if it has not been saved, and the panel will exit edit mode.

Entrance Tests

Selecting the Entrance Test tab at the bottom of the main window opens the Entrance Test data viewer for the selected applicant. By clicking on the "Edit" button, the user is able to adjust the data for this applicant. By pressing the "Save" button, the system checks if the information is correct. If all the information is correct, the system writes the information to the applicants' database by calling the stored SQL-procedure. Otherwise, the system generates pop-up windows (displayed on the screen) with a message stating which of the entered information does not satisfy the conditions of validation. The user is then asked to modify the entry panel, and the verification process is repeated. If a different entrant is selected, the information entered will be lost if it has not been saved, and the panel will exit edit mode.

Individual Achievements

This is a table with information on the applicant's individual achievements. The first column shows the "Name of Achievement" represented by a drop-down list, the second column shows the "score," and the third column shows the "supporting document," which is available for viewing and editing. If the information has not yet been entered, the table is empty. By default, of all the functionality, the user has the option to edit. If you click this button, the table becomes active, as well as the "Add new achievement" and "Save" and "Delete" buttons. If you press the "Add new achievement" button, a new empty row is added to the table. Select the desired achievement from the drop-down list in the "Name" field (the values are taken from the corresponding database directory of individual achievements). The score for the individual achievement is then entered. If necessary, you can attach a document confirming this individual achievement; for this purpose, there are two buttons "Edit" and "View" in the third field of the Confirmation document table. When you click on "Edit," a form appears where you can enter information about the document; when you click on "View," a similar form appears with fields that cannot be changed. When a contest group is deleted, a corresponding deletion is made in the database, and the tab is updated.

Competition Groups

The competition groups tab is a collapsed panel with information on the applicant's competition groups. When clicked, the tab opens and displays additional information on this applicant's competition category, which can be edited or deleted using the corresponding buttons. New information can only be entered by a specialist who has access to the relevant components of the applicants' database. To save the data, press the "Save" button. The system checks if the entered information is correct. If this check is successful, the system writes information to the applicants' database by calling the appropriate stored SQL-procedure, and the tab with the applicants' competition groups is updated. Otherwise, the system generates pop-up windows with an error message. When you click the "Delete" button, a window appears to confirm the deletion of the applicant's competition group. If yes is selected, it is deleted in the database and disappears from the screen.

There is a button, Add New Competition Group, that when clicked, a pop-up window will appear in which you can fill in all the required information. To confirm the information entered, click on the "Save" button, and then a check is made to ensure that the fields have been filled in correctly.

Additional Information

The tab contains a short list of additional information about the applicant in tabular form. If the information has not yet been entered, the table is empty. By default, of all the functionality, the user has the option to edit. The table and "Add" and "Save" and "Delete" buttons become active as soon as you press this button. If you press the "Add" button, a new empty row is added to the table. In the "Category" field, select the required information category from the drop-down list (values are taken from the relevant database reference). If you click on "Edit" the form in which you can enter information will appear; if you click on "View," the similar form with fields which are not available for change will appear. When deleting, a corresponding deletion is made in the database, and the tab is updated.

Grounds for 100 Points, Quotas, Preferential Rights

The tab contains a tabular summary of the additional information about the applicant in terms of special entry rights. If the information has not yet been entered, the tables in all three boxes are empty. By default, the user has the ability to edit all of the functionality. If you press this button, the table becomes active, as well as "Add" and "Save" and "Delete" buttons. The behavior of the tab is similar to the tab with Additional information on the applicant described above.

The advantage of the given solution is its adaptability—due to the fact that each tab of the interface is constructed in real time and is linked to the structure of the corresponding communication table and its query. This adaptivity is achieved by using an approach based on the separation of the MCU at the object-relational model level and the ICU at the interface level (DSL).

The Java language is used to develop the system, and JavaFX elements are used to design the corresponding MCCs of the DSL. In this case, in accordance with JavaFX logic, each template (MCC) has its own handler that contains a set of methods required to process the corresponding MCC and its behavior.

This results in the following structure of the MCC at the interface level and their handlers (Fig. 5.26).

Each handler has an identical set of methods in its structure, *getFieldData( )*, to retrieve a value from the corresponding MCC; *setFieldData(String data)*, to set the value of the corresponding MCC; and *setParameters(String originalNameOfField, String nameOfField)*, to set the MCC field with the name of the corresponding MCC field of the object-relational model, and a set of methods to scale the corresponding MCC in the interface tab. A more detailed code fragment of the MCC int/integer field handler is presented in Appendix A.

It should be noted that this uniform structure of the MCCs and their handlers allows the construction of a single matching function that determines which MCCs should be added to the interface tab if the corresponding MCU of the object-relational model is found. The full code of this handler is presented in Appendix B.

In this case, as there is more than one field displayed on a tab, all of them are written to a corresponding list, each element of which is then analyzed for correspondence with the MCC of the DSL. If there is a match, the appropriate DSM MCU is added to the interface, and the JavaFX FXML template loader is used, as the MCCs have been defined in terms of this tool.

It is important to note that if the structure of the communication table changes, then the display of the interface tab will also change according to the changes made. This versatility is achieved by linking the ICC interface to data types rather than to the structure of the tables, which may change. In order to provide this functionality, the system has a corresponding module discussed in the next section.

Fig. 5.26 Set of MCCs of
the GUI interface and their
handlers

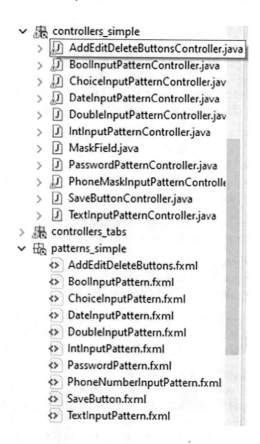

5.3.6 Design and Implementation of the DSL Evolution Module

Since the development of the DSL is carried out in full compliance with the proposed projection methodology, all levels of the DSL structure are consistent with each other as well as with the semantic model of the domain. As a consequence, it is possible to implement evolution at all levels of the DSL with the possibility of transferring these modifications to other levels, including the level of the semantic model of the domain. It is important to note that this modification is carried out automatically on the basis of the ICC and ICE previously allocated and requires the implementation of a separate module that allows separating the functionality to work with the system from the functionality to modify the functionality in use.

In our case, such an evolution module is designed to interact directly with the object-relational model of the domain, with the ability to change the sets of fields and tables of this model. In this case, since we have already highlighted the rules for cross-model transformations between DSM and all DSL layers, we only need to implement the interface components to access the relevant evolution scenarios, both vertical and horizontal.

In this case, we consider evolution scenarios in the general form presented earlier in Sect. 3.2. Accordingly, the evolution module must support both vertical and horizontal evolution of the DSL, so the following functionality must be provided in it (taking into account that we are considering an object-relational model):

- creating a new table (either from scratch, by defining a set of fields, or by copying existing ones);
- deleting an existing table;
- splitting one of the tables into several linked tables;
- merging several tables into one.

In the case of the horizontal evolution of the model, however, functionality must be provided to change the set of constituent tables, i.e., the fields:

- renaming a table field;
- adding a new table field;
- deleting an existing table field.

This set of operations is complete and allows all kinds of evolution (as shown in Sects. 3.2 and 3.3) of the object-relational model to be organized. Let's take a closer look at the interface that allows the implementation of each individual functionality.

Creating a New Table

If you create a table in the basic version, you need to set its basic attributes: name and list of fields. At the same time, for each field, its name and domain are selected (Fig. 5.27).

Once all the column names and domains as well as the table name are set, pressing the "Save" button will process the set table structure and create it in the object-relational model.

If the table has been successfully created, an appropriate message will be displayed. It is important to note that the table created will not be linked to existing tables in the object-relational model. Linking will need to be done later via a suitable interface tool, adding link fields to the other tables.

Copy the Table

If it is possible to create a new table using a template of existing tables, an additional interface is used (Fig. 5.28). In this case, the name of the new table must be set and the base table on which it will be created. The base table may be more than one—then all required existing tables are selected in sequence, and the fields to be copied into the new table are marked.

Once all the fields have been selected, clicking on the "Copy" button will run the script to create a new table. The selected columns of the new table will be checked for inconsistencies. If any contradictions are found, the corresponding window will be displayed to notify you of the need to make changes to the columns (Fig. 5.29).

To resolve conflicts, the user enters an interface similar to that of table editing (Fig. 5.27), where the user can correct the conflicting columns. Once all conflicts

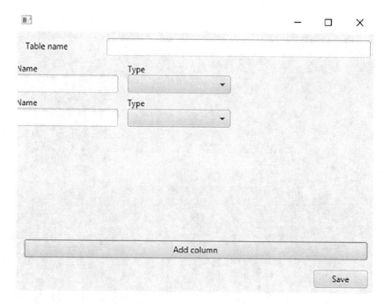

Fig. 5.27   Table creation interface

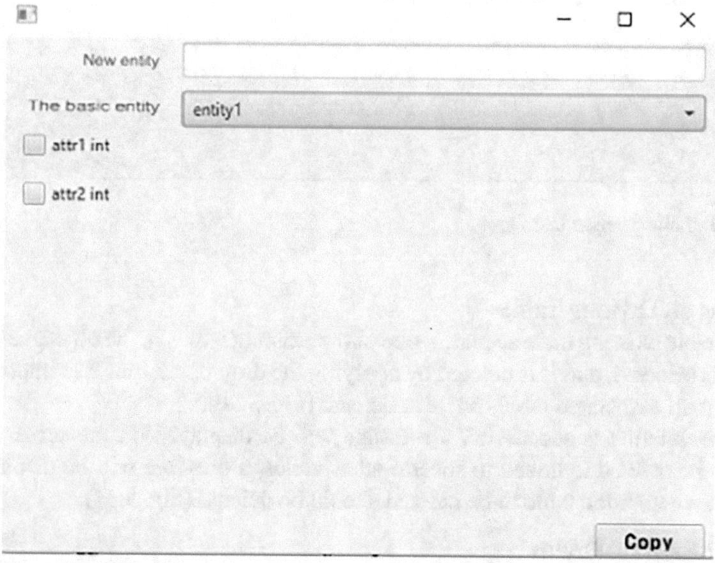

Fig. 5.28   Copy table interface

have been resolved by the user, a new table will be created. All information from the columns of the selected base tables will be moved to the new table.

In this way, not only the structure of the table will be created but also its contents. This will not contradict the structure of the table created earlier.

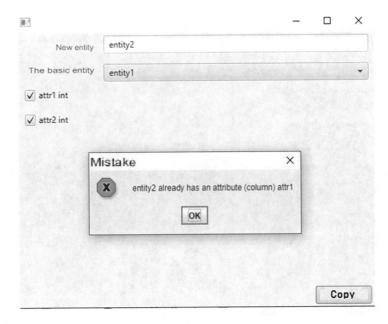

Fig. 5.29 Conflict window when copying a table

Fig. 5.30 Table deletion interface

Deleting an Existing Table

In the delete existing table scenario, one of the existing tables in the object-relational model is selected, and it is deleted by applying the drop operation. It is important to note that all associated tables are also deleted (Fig. 5.30).

If the deletion is successful, a message will be displayed on the screen. If the table to be deleted is linked to several other tables, a message will be displayed to confirm whether the table to be deleted should be deleted (Fig. 5.31).

Editing Existing Tables

When editing an existing table, it is possible both to change the set of existing attributes and to define new ones, including the possibility of their automatic filling based on existing data. It is also possible to rename table fields via this interface or delete them (this checks whether the field is an external key in other tables—in this case, both the original field and all related fields are deleted).

For example, you can add a new column to an existing one (Fig. 5.32).

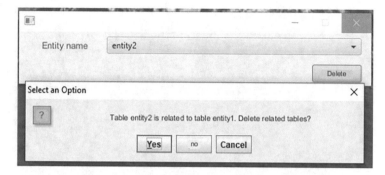

Fig. 5.31 Dialogue box when deleting linked tables

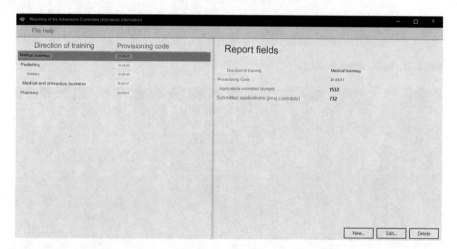

Fig. 5.32 Initial status of the table by training area

This is done using the following interface, where you can both add new attributes (columns) and calculating formulas on them (Fig. 5.33).

The output is the following target state of the table (Fig. 5.34).

5.3.7   Analysis of the Effectiveness of the Proposed Solution

As shown earlier (Fig. 5.32), the functional prototype for the Admissions Office includes all the functionality needed to make changes both to the object-relational data model used in the Admissions campaign process and to the associated interfaces. An important advantage of the proposed solution is the possibility to organize the evolution of the whole system (DSL as a whole and all system interfaces) in real time: users make changes through the relevant interface elements,

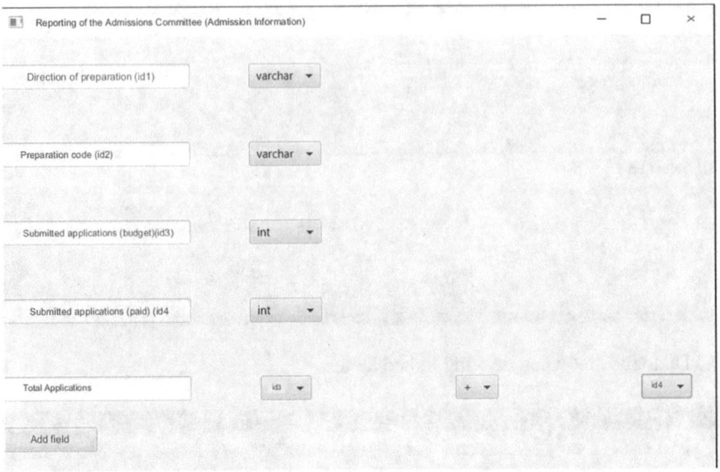

Fig. 5.33 Table editing interface

Fig. 5.34 Target state of the table by training area

without having to recreate the prototype as a whole, which makes the proposed solution a flexible tool for organizing the evolution of the subject area. For example, the user can change a set of attributes in already existing tables (Fig. 5.35).

When specifying a new set of attributes, it is possible to specify them either manually or based on the existing attributes of other tables. In this case (Fig. 5.36), for example, we expand the attribute set of the table with basic information on Applicants with an application code attribute.

As a result, the new field is immediately displayed on the interface (Fig. 5.37) and is available to the user for completion and editing (Fig. 5.38).

Since all changes are based on interconnected rules that implement a consistent evolution of all levels of the DSL and DSM, each such change to the system leads to a consistent change in all levels of the system. This eliminates the need to modify

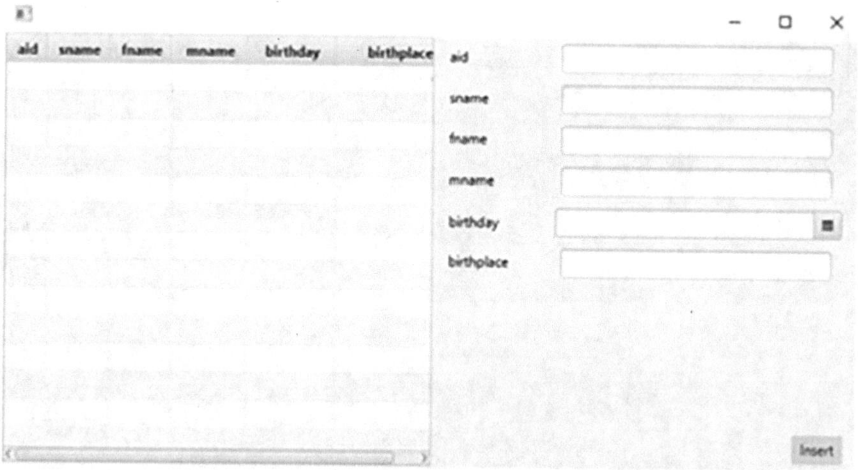

Fig. 5.35 Status of the Entrants table before the change

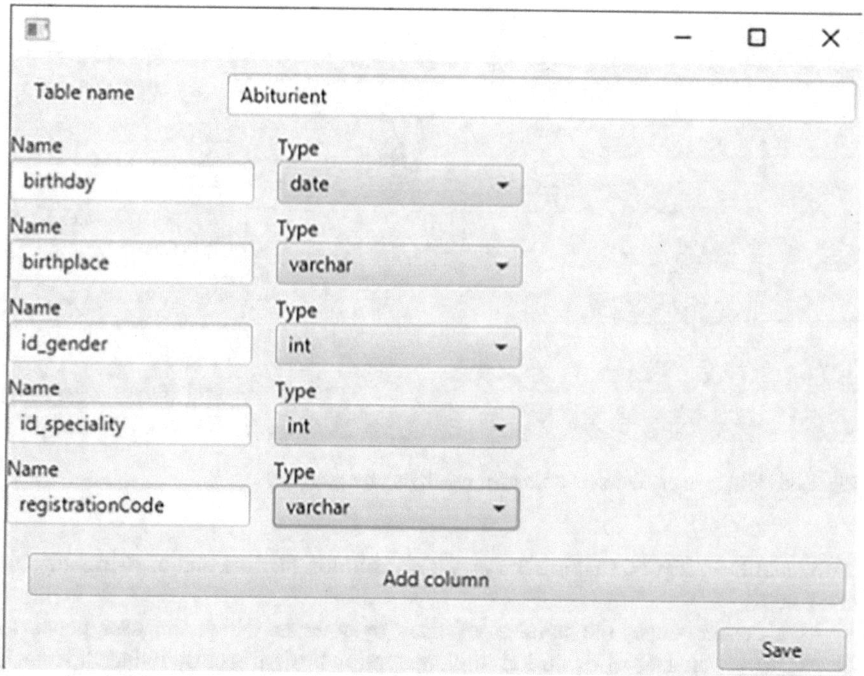

Fig. 5.36 Interface to changing a set of table attributes

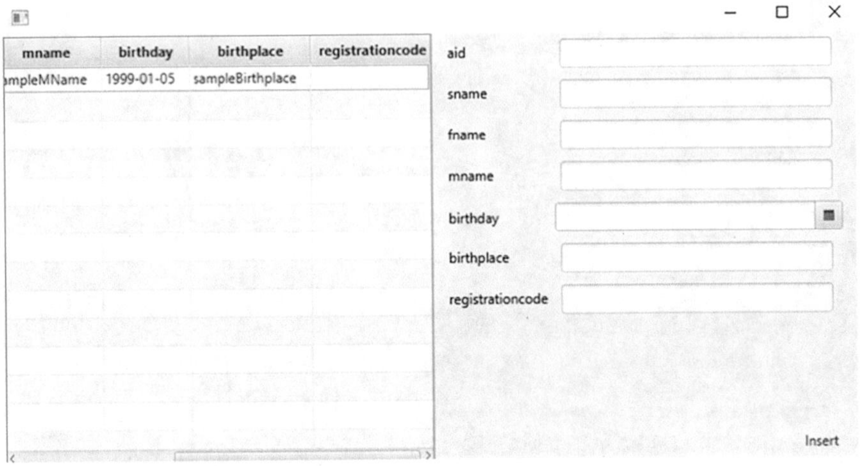

Fig. 5.37 Totals status of the Entrants table

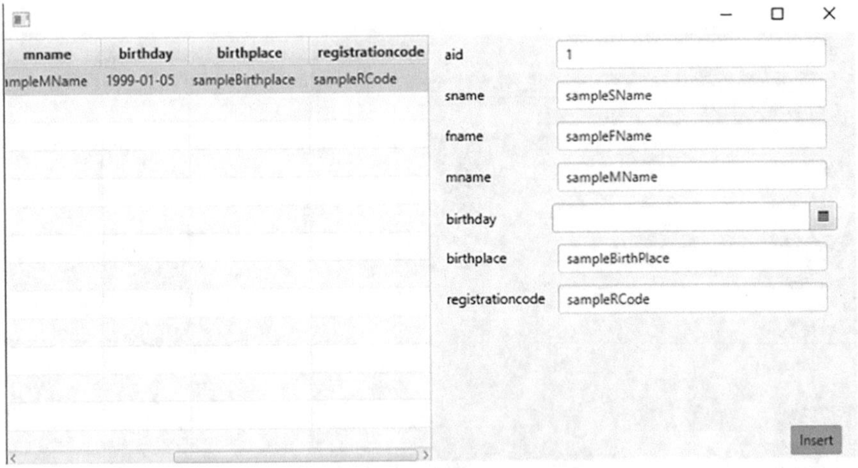

Fig. 5.38 Filling in the Entrants table after modifying the structure

individual DSL layers, making the proposed solution flexible and user-friendly for end users.

As a consequence, the number of lines of code in which the user needs to make changes in case of evolution implementation is significantly reduced. In fact, whereas previously changes had to be implemented at all levels of the source code (DSL as a whole), thanks to the proposed solution, all changes are carried out through an interface and do not require access to the source code.

For example, in the case of the above changes to change the structure of the Applicant table, the total number of lines of code added was 479. Without the proposed approach, all these rows would have to be entered manually, but with the proposed system, they are all generated automatically without any intervention from the end user.

5.4 Technical Features of the Implemented Software Prototypes

Since a similar set of technologies and tools were used to implement the software prototypes, we will present them in this single section.

The following hardware and system limitations must be met for both software prototypes to run:

- Intel Core i3+ processor, clocked at 1.8+GHz;
- DDR3+ 2+GB RAM;
- GDDR2+ 1+GB video memory;
- MS Word and Excel software package;
- Windows 7+ operating system;
- Java version 8.0+;
- PostgreSQL 12+ or similar.

Both prototypes were implemented using the Java language. This language was chosen because it is the main language in the case of the Eclipse XText software development environment [113] and plug-ins.

The total volume of the source code of the software prototype of the "Admissions Office" subject area is 11,479 lines, "Railway Station"—11,004 lines.

The set of Eclipse plug-ins and third-party open source libraries described earlier in Sect. 5.2.5 were also used to implement the DSL evolution processes. This set of plug-ins allows not only to technically define the elements of DSL evolution in terms of cross-model transformations but also to scale the built solution to other subject areas.

To implement the model transformation rules themselves, the graph (model) transformation language ATL was used [7]. The main advantages of this language were mentioned earlier in Sect. 4.2.3.

5.5 Analysis of the Applicability of the Proposed Approaches and Implemented Software Prototypes

Summarizing the results of the assessment of the characteristics of the proposed software environments according to ISO 25010-2015 [47], we obtain compliance of the built software environments with the following criteria: functionality, reliability, usability, efficiency, mobility, maintainability, and portability.

In terms of functionality, the following quality criterion can be highlighted:

- *Suitability*—demonstrated on various cases implemented using both software environments; the solutions presented have been tested;
- *Correctness*—the results obtained during the operation of the software environments were checked and evaluated by subject matter experts. In addition, the validation of the software environments was verified using archive data, after which the results were evaluated against the archive reference value. As a result of these experiments in the case of the Admission Board (the comparison was made on 183 indicators), the results coincided in 100% of cases; in the case of the trains distribution railway station (the comparison was made in the process of playing 54 experiments, in each case from 1 to 100 trains arriving to the station were considered), the deviation from the reference value was found in 3 experiments, but this deviation was caused by the fact that the proposed system could not find the solution within time which was given for solution search (this time coincides with the time of the search). However, in general, the solution found by the software (found after the allotted time) coincided with the reference.
- *Interoperability*—in this case we consider only the ability to interact with the user, which the built software environments fully enable as the interaction takes place through graphical human-machine interfaces.
- *Consistency*—the built software environments were developed in full compliance with the current Admission Regulations (in case of the Admission Board) and Standards and Guidelines for Freight Transport and Management of Freight Complexes of Railway Stations (in case of the Railway Station), which allows to confirm the consistency of the built solutions. Furthermore, the evolution modules implemented in both software environments will also allow future changes to the software environments in accordance with changes in these documents while maintaining compliance with consistency requirements.
- *Security*—the security of the built software environments is not part of this study, so in this case, we can only state the security of the built software environments provided by standard means: separation of data and access interfaces to them, protection of the data used at the server level with the database, etc. Thus, the security of the built software environments is satisfactory.

As we can see, in terms of functionality, the built software solutions meet most of the presented criteria: suitability, correctness, interoperability, and consistency. As a consequence, it can be concluded that the methods used in the development of the presented software environments allow building software solutions for which it is important to ensure a high degree of consistency with existing standards and constraints of the subject area, providing interaction with the end user. However, they are not applicable when it comes to the development of so-called mission-critical systems, for which the security indicator is critical.

In terms of reliability, the following quality criterion can be highlighted:

- *Stability*—both of the considered software environments provide the possibility to validate user scenarios, both at the input stage (checking the used constructs) and at the execution stage (searching for conflicts). However, the DSL evolution module of both environments requires manual control by the user (in particular, for compliance with the subject area in case of adding new entities). In addition, in the case of a railway station, the system has limitations on the number of users running scenarios simultaneously—no more than 15 users. In the case when the number of concurrent users exceeded this limit, hangups occurred in the system, and some of the scenarios did not have time to be processed. Thus, it can be stated that the level of compliance of the software environment to this quality criterion is satisfactory.

- *Resilience to errors*—both built software environments have built-in mechanisms for checking user scenarios, both at the input stage (checking the constructs used) and at the runtime stage (searching for conflicts). As a consequence, it can be argued that the built systems are robust to errors.

In this way, the constructed systems meet the reliability criteria sufficiently, being robust against errors. However, this is not sufficient for using the presented approaches in the case of high-loaded and high-performance systems, for which the organization of simultaneous access of a large number of users (more than 50) and processing of a large number of requests in real time is critical.

Similar conclusions can be drawn when analyzing the compliance of the presented software environments with the performance criteria:

- *Nature of change over time* and *Nature of change in resources*—from the point of view that any modification of the language constructs and its metamodel leads to increased complexity of processing these constructs, the proposed methods provide only satisfactory compliance with this quality criterion. However, as shown above, this becomes critical only when more than 15 users are working with the system and part of the scenarios remain unprocessed in the allotted time. In the case of fewer users, even after modifying the language constructs and adding new entities, the transaction processing time changed by an average of 1.3ms (in the case of the railway station case).

In terms of usability, however, the software environments developed are of high quality as they fulfil the following criteria:

- *Understandability* and *Trainability*—the developed software environments are fully based on the formal ontology which determines terminology and semantic model of the subject area and, as a consequence, are understandable to the end users. It is important to note that in the case of both software environments, no separate training activities were necessary, which confirms the high degree of compliance with the criteria of understandability and teachability.
- *Ease of use*—Scenarios in the case of the railway station DSL are formulated using commands applicable to the subject area, thereby ensuring that these scenarios are easy to create. In the case of the Admission Board, on the other hand, all interaction takes place via graphical interfaces, which also greatly simplifies the ability to generate various reports on the admission campaign and the entry of information on applicants.

In terms of maintainability, the presented software environments allow for real-time modifications and meet the following criteria:

- *Modifiability* and *Testability*—both environments contain separate modules for organizing the evolution of the DSL, providing the possibility to modify its structures through the interface in real time, without the need to make manual changes. Thus, in the case of modifying the main structure of the Admissions Committee-Applicant module (adding an additional attribute), the total number of lines of code added was 479. Without the proposed approach, all these lines would have to be entered manually, in the case of the proposed system, all of them are generated automatically without end user intervention. The changes made are immediately available to the end user, so they can be checked for correctness immediately, indicating that the changes made are easy to test.

Thus the approaches presented can be applied to the development of systems (and the DSL for such systems) for which it is important to support easy and rapid changes without the need for manual modification at the source code level.

Finally, in terms of mobility and portability, the systems built meet the following criteria:

- *Adaptability* and *Conformability*—similar to conformability of changeability, the built software environments provide a high degree of adaptability of the built solutions in real time and ensure that the various provisions and constraints of the subject area remain conformable. In this context, it is also important to note the cross-platform (and therefore portability) of the built solutions, as the Java language was used in their development.

In this way, the built software environments provide a high degree of adaptability. As a consequence, the approaches used in their development can be applied to the construction of other systems for which ease of change (adaptability) and compliance with the existing constraints (and regulations) of the subject area are required.

To summarize the presented analysis of the quality of the built software environments, it can be argued that the approaches, methods, and algorithms used in their development can also be applied in the case of building general purpose adaptive systems. However, it is not recommended to use them for high-load, high-performance, demanding systems, in which it is important to ensure a high level of security and system performance in the case of a large number of simultaneous users and requests.

Chapter 6
Discussion and Further Development

Abstract This chapter presents a further development of the approach proposed and its application to more complex decision-making problems in dynamic contexts. In this case, an important aspect of problem-solving is the use of ontologies that allow not only describing the domain entities and relationships between them but also domain constraints, which are the basis for taking into account various assessments of decision-makers.

6.1 Crisisology-Based Trade-Off Optimization in Sociotechnical Systems

Over the past decades, production in general and software engineering in particular were understood and practiced in different ways. Changeable business constraints, complex technical requirements, and the so-called human factors imposed on the software solutions caused what was articulated as "software crises."

In software development, a crisis is a disproportion between client's expectations and the actual product behavior. Such crises typically result from an imbalance between available resources, business requirements, and technical constraints. These complex sources of trouble require a multifaceted approach (as well as a related software) to address each of their layers.

The idea to manage the crisis is to make the digital product development (DPD) process sustainable by design. In certain cases, "manage" may actually mean different things such as respond to, adjust to, mitigate, conquer, etc. To implement this, the digital product should meet certain quality level. To be more precise, this overall quality is a balanced combination of certain sub-qualities, generally known as quality attributes (QAs). Obviously, these QAs are often contradictory. A typical example would be security and performance: promoting security inhibits performance and vice versa. Therefore, to ensure/guarantee that a certain QA combination is really well balanced, trade-off analysis and management are required. At this point, optimization comes into play. Multi-criteria choice of alternatives in IT system architecture facilitates sustainable development of the application domain.

© The Author(s), under exclusive license to Springer Nature Switzerland AG 2024   111
E. Babkin, B. Ulitin, *Ontology-Based Evolution of Domain-Oriented Languages*,
https://doi.org/10.1007/978-3-031-42202-7_6

The general idea of the research scheme within the framework of crisisology is presented as follows:

1. identification of key BTH factors (business, technology, human)
2. categorization of factors and establishment of dependencies (category theory)
3. description of factors and dependencies in the object language
4. primary "rough" optimization (AHP, ACDM/ATAM, etc.) with semiautomatic evaluation and ranking of alternatives
5. secondary "fine" optimization (if required)
6. immersion in an applied object environment based on a virtual machine (VM based on category/combinator theory)
7. final search for the optimal solution (DSS)

However, the most important limitation for the application of this scheme is the fact that the proposed assessments of various factors by experts are often not formalized but in the form of linguistic information that requires further processing.

In what follows, we will focus on the description of a method for a linguistic-based multi-criteria choice of alternatives in IT system architecture. We also propose a software service that allows the users processing such assessments in a linguistic form to make a multi-criteria decision on the use of DPD in the enterprise's processes.

6.2   Crisisology as a Conceptual Framework for Multi-criteria Decision Support in Information Systems Design

As we mentioned before, in their processes, enterprises use various types of information systems. Once a system is designed, organizations spring up around its structures. In a very real sense, technical designs beget organizations for better or worse. Eliminating or adding organizations that support systems or elements of systems can have very real impact to the structure of a system that is built or in the process of being built. Given the large number of alternative information systems, the most difficult for the enterprise is the stage of choosing the target system, based on BTH factors.

At the same time, the description of the system and reviews about it are often not enough to assess the human factors. If the assessment of the technical capabilities of the system and the financial costs of its implementation can be automated to some extent, then taking into account user requirements is a nontrivial process.

User requirements are formulated in the form of linguistic assessments, while each user can use his own system of criteria for assessment (compare bad-good-excellent and slow-fast). The main task is to take into account all the necessary assessments, expressed in a heterogeneous form, when making the final decision on a system.

There are certain attempts to solve this problem in the literature and the practical environment. For example, Martínez et al. offer a generalized decision-making model based on linguistic information with the help of an operator that takes into account the number of matching and non-matching expert assessments. Reference [19] provides a system prototype that allows users to enter linguistic scores without modification. However, this system involves preliminary work in the form of creating a single "terminological" base for experts and ranking all available assessments using unified principles.

As a result, these solutions are highly specialized and still require a certain unification of the rating systems of various users. What is more crucial, both solutions contradict the fact that experts can evaluate different criteria using different scales, selected individually for each of them.

To solve this problem, in the following sections, we describe a multi-criteria selection system based on dynamic interfaces. The proposed system allows for each user (or groups of users) to define their own system of evaluation criteria (in linguistic form) with their own gradation scales for these evaluations. This approach makes it possible to unify the procedure for making a decision on the choice of an information system while not requiring the introduction of a unified system (and scale) of assessment.

6.3   A Proposed Method for Hierarchical Multi-criteria Choice

There are numerous attempts to elaborate new decision-making approaches or adopt existing ones to real-life cases, like healthcare, performance evaluation of partnerships, fiber composites optimization, reverse logistics evaluation, project resources scheduling, supplier selection, and aircraft incident analysis. Usually, traditional approaches like TOPSIS, ELECTRE, and VIKOR are used.

The considerable drawback is that these methods rely mostly on quantitative evaluations, even given in a form of fuzzy sets. On the other hand, estimations that are given by experts during problem discussion can be both quantitative and qualitative. Qualitative evaluations become more and more preferable in complex situations because compared to quantitative evaluations, qualitative ones have the serious advantage of their ability to express fuzzy information (e.g., hesitation). However, according to our rigorous analysis of the field, there is an emerging trend of combining traditional decision-making approaches with methods of processing qualitative evaluations. The combination of TOPSIS methodology and 2-tuple model for analyzing qualitative assessments represents a bright example.

Reliable and flexible means for analysis of qualitative evaluations are provided within the scientific area of "linguistic decision-making" and "linguistic multi-attribute decision-making." These and other methods of processing qualitative evaluations now are generally called "computing with words," among which the most popular are:

- linguistic computational model based on membership functions
- linguistic symbolic computational model based on ordinal scales
- max-min operators, linguistic symbolic computational model based on convex combinations

In many cases, information that comes from the experts is heterogeneous due to its multigranularity, and there are approaches (and methods) to work with such information: the fusion approach for managing multigranular linguistic information, the linguistic hierarchy approach, and the method of extended linguistic hierarchies.

It is important to emphasize that existing approaches concentrate either on analysis of only quantitative or qualitative assessments. Very few approaches focus on both types of estimations. At the same time, modern methodologies are likely to assume that there are a number of experts without capturing the area of their expertise as well as the fact that criteria also belong to different abstraction levels (BTH in our case). More importantly, existing methods for decision-making are demonstrated on artificial cases with very few experts and alternative solutions. This brings us to the point where we propose a new methodology that could incorporate most of the gaps described above.

We call our approach multilevel multi-attribute linguistic decision-making (ML-MA-LDM). The proposed approach consists of several consecutive steps starting from defining the estimation rules and finishing with the communication stage. It is important to note that these steps can be found individually in various papers describing the decision-making process, but never were fused in a consistent way. The proposed approach includes:

1. Setting up rules for providing estimations and distribution of criteria weights. In the proposed approach, we make several assumptions:

   a. experts give honest evaluations;
   b. experts believe each other;
   c. experts choose granularity of evaluations according to their experience and knowledge about a problem;
   d. experts have the same understanding of evaluations;

2. Defining available linguistic sets, a context-free grammar, and transformation function;
3. Multi-level definition of the desired state, criteria, and alternatives: (a) analyzing the desired state on each level of abstraction; (b) formulating criteria for each level of abstraction; (c) formulating alternatives.
4. Giving multilevel and multi-criteria evaluations: (a) aggregating information; (b) searching for the best alternative; (c) communicating the solution found.

After criteria and alternatives were defined, all experts start giving evaluations of each alternative for each available criterion. Let $x = \{x_1, x_2, \ldots, x_N\}$ be the list of alternatives, $c = \{c_1, c_2, \ldots, c_M\}$ the list of criteria, and $e = \{e_1, e_2, \ldots, e_T\}$ the list of experts. We assume that each expert e_k can evaluate alternatives using different linguistic scales S_{g_k} with granularity g_k. In the case of comparative evaluations, we also have the grammar G_H, which can be also used for creation of linguistic evaluations. Moreover, the criteria are given for each level of abstraction in the meta-decision framework, i.e., let $l = \{l_1, l_2, \ldots, l_Z\}$ be the list of the levels of abstraction. Therefore, one evaluation for each given alternative is obtained, and the best alternative can be found by sorting these evaluations according to rules of comparing hesitant 2-tuple fuzzy sets.

As a result, for each expert, we get a matrix of evaluations $R_k = \left(T_{S_{g_k}}^{ij} \right)_{N \times M}$, where $T_{S_{g_k}}^{ij}$ —an evaluation of the expert e_k for the i-th alternative on the j-th criterion in the format of HFLTS on the scale S_g.

Then, it is important to find an accumulated evaluation for combination of each alternative i, every level of abstraction l, and every expert e_k by aggregating evaluations for every criterion corresponding to the given abstraction level. Then for each expert, we get the following matrix: $T_j^i = MHTWA_{S_{g_k}}^p \left(T_{S_{g_k}}^v \right), c_v \in l_j$, where i is the index of alternative; j the index of the abstraction level; and p the vector of criteria weights, $p = (p_1, p_2, \ldots, p_M)^T$, $p_j \geq 0$, $\sum_{j=1}^{M} p_j = 1$. Here we propose to use the MHTMA operator because each criterion has its own defined weight. So, for each expert, we get the following decision matrix: $R_k = \left(T_{S_{g_k}}^{ij} \right)_{N \times Z}$.

The next step should be aggregation of evaluations for each level of abstraction separately. From the previous step, we get T matrices with evaluations, each of size $N \times Z$. In order to make aggregation for each level of abstraction, we need to have Z matrices with evaluations, each of the size $N \times T$, where N is a number of alternatives and T is a number of criteria. So, for each abstraction level, we get the following decisions matrix: $R_U = \left(T_{S_{g_k}}^{ij} \right)_{N \times T}$.

After previous stages, the total evaluation is calculated for each level of abstraction l_u, for each i-th alternative, and for each expert given. If w is the given vector of experts' weights, $w = (w_1, w_2, \ldots, w_T)^T$, $w_j \geq 0$, $\sum_{j=1}^{T} w_j = 1$, then for each level of abstraction, we get the following matrix: $T_j^i = MHTWA_{S_{g_k}}^w \left(T_{S_{g_k}}^{i_1}, T_{S_{g_k}}^{i_2}, \ldots, T_{S_{g_k}}^{i_t} \right)$, where i is the index of the alternative and j the index of the abstraction level.

If the vector of weights is not given, the following formula should be used for their calculation:

$$m(i) = \begin{cases} w, i = 1 \\ \left(1 - \sum_{j=1}^{i-1} w \right) \times w, 1 \leq i \leq T \\ 1 - \sum_{j=1}^{i-1} w, i = x \end{cases} \tag{6.1}$$

where $w \in$ is the proportion of the first expert's evaluation in the weights' sum. Therefore, we get the following decisions matrix: $R_k = \left(T_{S_{g_k}}^{ij} \right)_{N \times Z}$.

Finally, the total evaluation for each i-th alternative and for each level of abstraction is found:

$T_i = MHTWA^q_{S_{g_k}} \left(T^{i1}_{S_{g_k}}, T^{i2}_{S_{g_k}}, \ldots, T^{iZ}_{S_{g_k}} \right)$, where i is the index of alternative and q the vector of weights of levels of abstraction, $q = (q_1, q_2, \ldots, q_Z)^T, q_j \geq 0$, $\sum_{j=1}^{Z} q_j = 1$. So, we get the following vector of evaluations $r = \left(T^i_{S_{g_k}} \right)_N$, where $T^i_{S_{g_k}}$ is the aggregated evaluation for i-th alternative in a form of HFLTS on the scale S_{g_k}.

As a result, we get assessments that draw insights on how each alternative is measured on each level of abstraction, and a decision-maker can use this information to better understand the scope of alternatives and their influence on each aspect of the problem situation. It can also be possible to customize a methodology at this point; for example, it is possible to select only a subset of levels of abstraction, which interests the decision-maker to make the final decision.

6.4   A Proposed Hierarchical Structure of the Criteria for Selection of IT System Architecture

The process of choosing an IT system architecture is rarely fast, as it determines the strategy for the development of the IT infrastructure of the enterprise for the next few years. In this chapter, we do not consider the decision-making process to automate the company business processes, considering that it has already been successfully completed, and it remains to decide on the IT system architecture itself.

In general, the architecture of any distributed IS consists of clients (user devices) and a more powerful server that clients access. Depending on the location of the components of the three layers of IS on the client and server, the following types of distributed architectures are distinguished: a *file-server* architecture, a *client-server* architecture (i.e., *two-tier* and *three-tier*), a *monolithic* architecture, a *microservice* architecture, and a *cloud* architecture. Each architecture has its own characteristics, advantages, and disadvantages, so it is extremely important to take into account all of them when choosing and making the best choice for the company, which will positively affect its KPIs.

When deciding on an architecture, we take into account both quantitative and qualitative factors, reflecting the opinion not only about the architecture as a whole but also about the experience of using it by other companies. Among these criteria, the following are the most significant:

- *Cost*. In most cases, the less that a product costs, the more attractive it is. This criterion is quantitative, and the evaluation scale is inversely proportional to its values.

- **Learning curve**. The easier it is to learn how to use, configure, install, and maintain a product, the more attractive it is. Therefore, low or shallow learning curves are given higher ratings, and steeper learning curves are given lower ratings.
- **Support**. Better support is more attractive and is therefore given higher ratings, and weaker support is given lower ratings.
- **Provider reputation**. The more solid the provider reputation, the higher the ratings.
- **Volatility**. A highly stable product with a long track record in the marketplace is given higher ratings than an emerging product.

In addition to these criteria, we can also consider criteria that allow us to assess the possible risks of implementing an architecture implementation project:

- **Schedule**. Describes the possible total delay in the project schedule (in days). The greater the possible delay, the less preferred the alternative.
- **Quality**. Serves to assess the impact of a potential decline in quality on the vital functions of the enterprise. The greater the assessment of a given risk, the less preferred the alternative.

Arbitrarily fractional (counting) scales can be used to evaluate the indicated criteria. Within the framework of this study, we will adhere to the following scales (Table 6.1, letter inside parentheses in Criterion category—type of BTH criterion).

In this case, the possibility of replacing the rating scale is important, as well as the use of not a single scale but its adaptation for each individual expert in accordance with the principles described in Sect. 6.3.

This is also fully consistent with object models (including in terms of category theory), which make it possible to define an integrated assessment as a categorical (multi-argument) valuation in various correlations.

Table 6.1 IT system architecture evaluation criteria evaluation scales

Criterion	Type	Scale
Cost (*B*)	Quantitative	
Learning curve (*H*)	Qualitative	None, complex, medium, simple, intuitive
Support (*T*)	Qualitative	None, under the contract, short-term, long-term
Provider reputation (*B*)	Qualitative	negative, indefinite, positive
Volatility (*B*)	Qualitative	Unstable, volatile, stable
Schedule (*B, T*)	Qualitative	10 segments: from 1 month to 0 days
Quality (*T*)	Qualitative	Worse than/comparable to//higher than/is the standard for analogues

6.5 Description of the Decision Support Service

In order to work with the criteria listed above and evaluate the architecture of IT systems according to them, we use a software prototype that includes a backend responsible for the ranking of alternatives and a frontend (GUI) necessary for setting all the components required for evaluation (hierarchy of evaluation criteria, alternatives, assessments of alternatives by experts, etc.). The architecture and operation of the prototype are shown in Fig. 6.1. As mentioned earlier, the first step in deciding on the choice of a particular information system is to determine the criteria for its selection.

At the same time, it is important to remember that the criteria, by their nature, can be presented in various forms: numerical, textual (linguistic), etc. At the same time, even numerical criteria may differ in assessment scales in terms of quality (from lower to higher and vice versa). Therefore, in the created service, the first stage is the creation of a system of criteria and the setting of scales for their evaluation.

In this case, the point under discussion is the method of presenting the criteria. The use of ontologies seems to be the most appropriate, since by setting a criterion, we also determine the restrictions associated with it. In addition, the criteria can be interconnected, which can also be described using the corresponding elements of the ontological model.

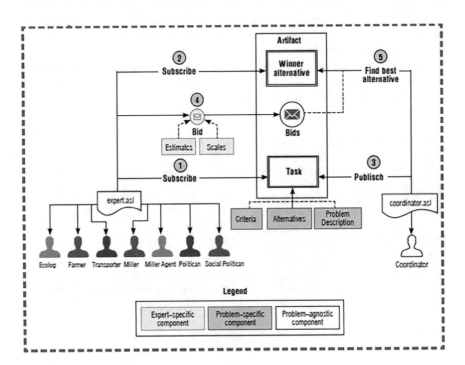

Fig. 6.1 Multi-agent architecture for multi-attribute LDM

Using the appropriate GUI (Fig. 6.2), the user is able to first determine the name of the criteria system and then the name of each individual criterion and select the most appropriate data type to represent it. In this case, the supported data types are selected based on the nature of the possible criteria for selecting information systems: *integer* (int) and *fractional* (float) *numbers*, to quantify information systems (e.g., allowable number of users); *date*, in the case of distinguishing newer information systems from older ones; and *textual* (varchar), to represent linguistic assessments. At the same time, a unique name within the criteria system is assigned for each criterion. What is more important, we can use not only the data types but full-fledged domains for each individual evaluation criterion, which is fully consistent with the general theory of categories, the main provisions of which are used in the approach proposed.

After the criteria are defined, they are saved. In this case, a database structure is created that corresponds structurally and in terms of types to the entered criteria. This is expedient, since the input of assessments on alternatives by experts must initially be stored in some structured form for subsequent transfer of the entire set of alternatives and assessments on them to the decision-making service (alternatives ranking).

And for these purposes, it is optimal to use an object-relation database (ORDB) structure, which allows both to prevent the input of values that are contradictory in

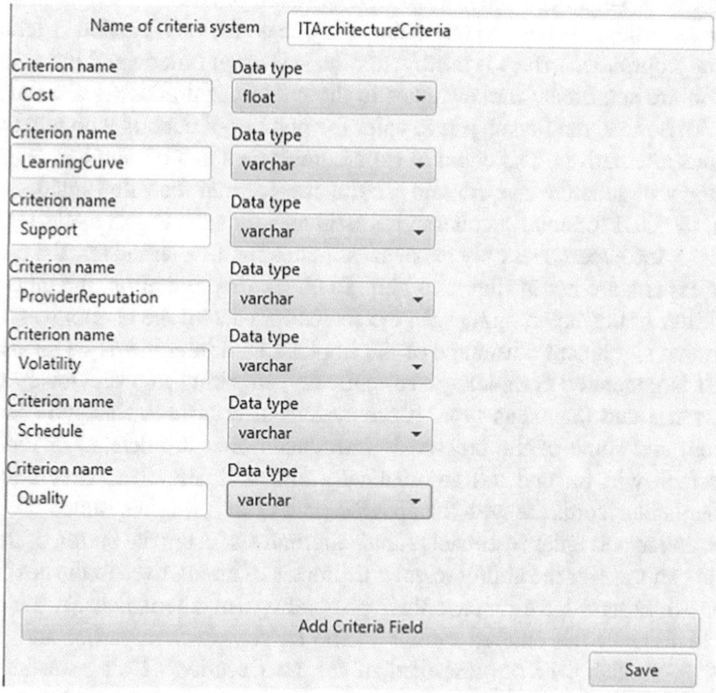

Fig. 6.2 GUI fragment for creating a criteria system

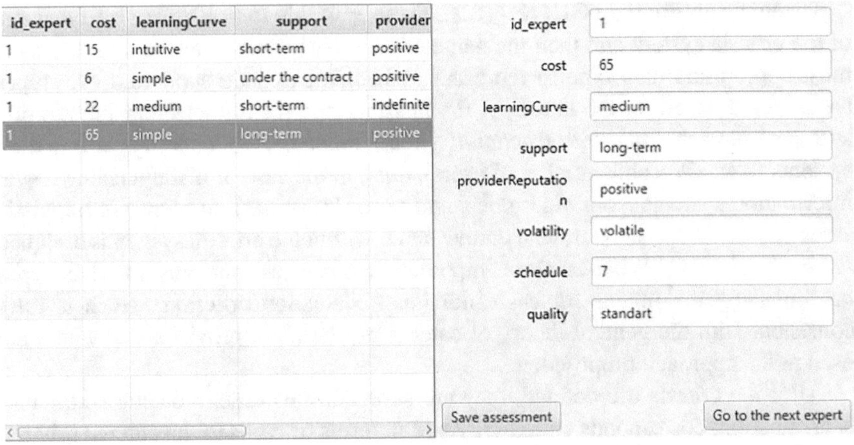

id_expert	cost	learningCurve	support	provider
1	15	intuitive	short-term	positive
1	6	simple	under the contract	positive
1	22	medium	short-term	indefinite
1	65	simple	long-term	positive

id_expert	1
cost	65
learningCurve	medium
support	long-term
providerReputation	positive
volatility	volatile
schedule	7
quality	standart

Save assessment   Go to the next expert

Fig. 6.3 GUI for entering alternatives by the experts

terms of type to the corresponding criteria and to save all assessments in the form of a single object (table). In addition, this type of database, in comparison with NoSQL solutions, has a higher performance and, at the same time, structurally corresponds to the previously identified structure of the hierarchy of assessments according to various criteria, each of which is a multidimensional object.

In the next step, we need to refine the rating scale for each created criterion. For this, an appropriate interface is used. After the system of criteria and the scale of its evaluation are set, the system switches to the mode of introducing alternatives by experts. To do this, the first step is to enter the number of experts who will evaluate the various alternatives. The count of experts must be a natural number. Otherwise, the system will generate an error and ask the user to enter the value again.

Next, the GUI for entering alternative estimates for each expert opens (Fig. 6.3). In this case, the expert sees only his own estimates for all alternatives, the estimates of other experts are not available to him. To check this limitation, the table shows the identifier of the expert along with the scores for each of the alternatives.

The most significant advantage of the implemented interface is its adaptability. The GUI is generated completely automatically, adjusting to a previously created set of criteria and their data type. If the system of criteria is changed (new ones are added, and some of the previously introduced ones are deleted or modified), the interface will be updated automatically and will allow the expert to make assessments in accordance with the updated state of the criteria system.

After one expert enters estimates for all alternatives, using the button of the same name, he can transfer the ability to enter estimates of alternatives to the next expert.

After all experts have entered their own ratings of alternatives, a button will appear to transfer the entered ratings to the service for comparing and ranking alternatives (which will be described in the next section). Data transfer in this case is carried out using a JSON package containing all the information necessary for evaluation: a set of criteria, evaluation scales for individual criteria, a set of alternatives, and the results of evaluation by experts of all alternatives.

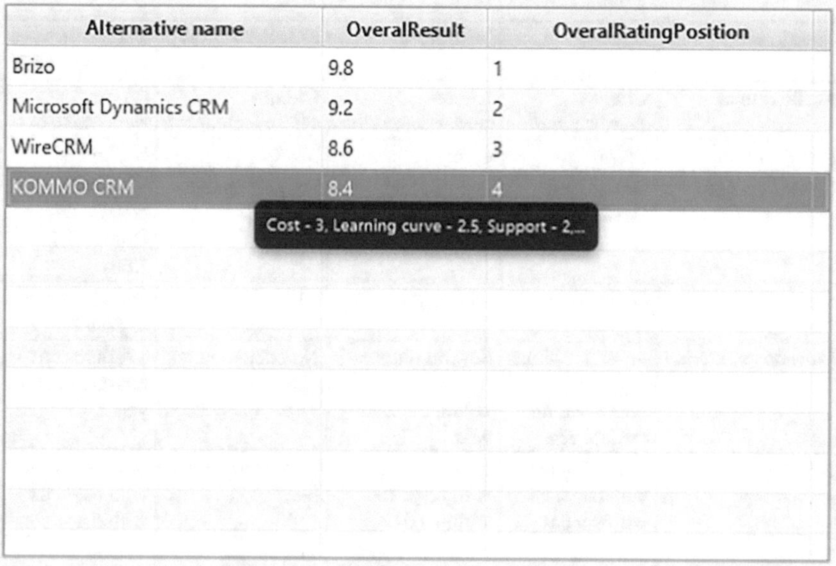

Alternative name	OveralResult	OveralRatingPosition
Brizo	9.8	1
Microsoft Dynamics CRM	9.2	2
WireCRM	8.6	3
KOMMO CRM	8.4	4

Cost - 3, Learning curve - 2.5, Support - 2,...

Fig. 6.4 GUI for displaying ranked alternatives

As a result of processing the package by the alternative evaluation service, a response JSON packet arrives containing ranked alternatives in descending order of their preference. This ranked set of alternatives is displayed on the screen using the appropriate interface component (Fig. 6.4). In this case, when selecting each individual alternative, the results of the assessment for each individual criterion are displayed.

6.6   Case Study of the Proposed Prototype

In order to demonstrate the application of the described approach and a software prototype, we will compare CPM systems for an enterprise. In this case, the main aspect of the comparison will concern the architecture of these systems in the context of the criteria described earlier.

To simplify, we restrict ourselves to four systems of this class: Brizo (a CRM system with advanced functionality for management accounting), WireCRM (a multifunctional platform like a "single window" for comprehensive control of business processes and interaction with customers), KOMMO CRM, and Microsoft Dynamics CRM (a set of intelligent applications divided into several areas). A summary of the features of the systems in the context of the previously identified criteria is given in Table 6.2.

Table 6.2 Brief description of the systems under consideration

Criterion	Brizo	WireCRM	KOMMO CRM	Microsoft Dynamics CRM
Architecture	**Client-server/cloud**	**Client-server/monolithic**	**Client-server/monolithic**	*Client-server/cloud*
Cost (per user)	15$/m	6$/m	22$/m	65$/m
Learning curve	Online Help Docs	Online Help Docs	Support Online Help Docs	Corporate courses Support Online Help Docs
Support	Online chat	Online chat	24/7	24/7, Personal assistant
Provider reputation	Several failures (up to 24 hours) within the last year	Several failures (up to 24 hours) within the last year	No open reports	1 failure (up to 2 hours) in the last year
Volatility	Several updates with bugs, fix within a day	Several updates with bugs, fix within a day	No updates, only fixes	Several updates with bugs, fix within a week
Schedule	No open reports	No open reports	The update release plan is published; the timing depends on the specific enterprise	The update release plan is published; the timing is fixed
Quality	10% negative reviews	10.6% negative reviews	1% negative reviews	6% negative reviews

Of course, the information given above can be interpreted differently by experts and lead to the fact that their assessments will differ according to identical criteria. In our case, we work with two experts who have expertise in the field of CPM systems and obtain the following estimates of alternatives represented in Table 6.3. For entering these values, the experts use GUI, described in Fig. 6.3 (the order of the rows in the table corresponds to the order of the columns with systems).

After all the ratings are entered, we send them for processing to the rating ranking service via a JSON file containing all the necessary information both on the alternatives and their evaluation criteria and on the specific values of the experts ratings.

In the response JSON file, we receive a ranked list of alternatives (Fig. 6.4). In this case, it can be seen that the system, in the course of comparing alternatives according to all criteria, chose Brizo as the optimal system and KOMMO CRM as the least optimal. At the same time, the discrepancies in expert estimates on such criteria as learning curve, volatility, and schedule had the greatest impact on the decision.

Table 6.3 Results of evaluation of alternatives by experts (1st expert/2nd expert)

Criterion	Brizo	WireCRM	KOMMO CRM	Microsoft Dynamics CRM
Cost	15/15	6/6	22/22	65/65
Learning curve	Intuitive/simple	Simple/simple	Medium/simple	Simple/medium
Support	Short-term/short-term	Under the contract/under the contract	Short-term/short-term	Long-term/long-term
Provider reputation	Positive/positive	Positive/positive	Indefinite/indefinite	Positive/positive
Volatility	Stable/volatile	Stable/volatile	Volatile/unstable	Volatile/volatile
Schedule	14/28	14/28	3/3	7/7
Quality	Higher/higher	Comparable/comparable	Comparable/worse	standart/standart

In this case, when ranking, we use the entire structure of the BTH criteria described earlier (Table 6.1), thereby obtaining a socio-technical (not purely technical) assessment.

Chapter 7
Conclusion and Final Remarks

Abstract At the end, we present a brief summary of the results obtained. A comparison of the obtained results with existing analogues is also given (both in terms of theoretical approaches and methods and practical tools). Finally, we present several ideas for further development of the study.

Thus, this research examined the development and evolution of subject-oriented interface modeling languages for general-purpose software systems in dynamic contexts. The aim of the study is to improve the efficiency of life cycle support processes for general-purpose software systems by developing new models and methods for the evolution of DSLs for interface modelling. The projection approach proposed in this work allows changing the structure of all layers of the DSL in real time without having to recreate the whole application. This is the main difference between the in-house solution and existing approaches [10, 25, 45, 55], the basic idea of which is to refuse to implement full evolution of the DSL in favor of recreating the structure of the language when it needs to be modified.

The scientific novelty of the study is as follows:

- Based on the analysis of existing approaches and methods for DSL development, a generalized model-based DSL structure is presented (Sect. 2.3), which is a unified representation of all levels of the DSL structure.
- The various types (models) of DSL evolution are formalized for the modelling of the human-machine interface for general-purpose software systems (Sect. 3.2), allowing the consistent evolution of the DSM and all levels of a DSL to be defined in accordance with the proposed projection approach.
- A set of cross-model transformations (based on graph transformations— presented in Sect. 3.3) is constructed and implemented to organize the horizontal and vertical evolution of external DSL modelling of general-purpose software system interfaces.
- On the basis of the identified system of cross-model transformations, a new method (called the projection approach) for external DSL development is proposed (Sect. 3.1), which allows to automate the DSL development process for modelling general-purpose software system interfaces and to use the results

of subject area analysis in DSL design and implementation, as well as to organize automated DSL evolution.
• Algorithmization (Sects. 3.2 and 3.3) and software implementation (Sects. 4.2 and 4.3) of the GUI transformation procedure as an example of an external DSL for two subject areas are carried out according to the proposed method.

As a part of the practical part of the work, prototypes of information environments for two subject areas have been implemented: "The software system of the University Admissions Committee" and "The software system of the railway station resource allocation." The built prototypes are based on the proposed projection approach, providing the user not only with the functionality to solve the tasks of the subject area but also to organize the coordinated evolution of all levels of DSLs and DSM.

In this case, the consistency of all models (from DSM to DSL syntax models) is achieved by using the appropriate model representation tools. So, at the level of working with DSM, ontologies are used, which make it possible to reflect not only the entities of the domain and the relationships between them but also the limitations of the domain. At the level of DSL models, representations consistent at the meta-model level (KM3 descriptions) are used, thereby allowing the use of cross-model transformations for transitions between models of different levels.

Thus, the universality of the proposed design approach is achieved, since it is formulated at the level of meta-models and can be adapted to various types of specific models of different levels.

In contrast to existing subject-oriented solutions for different domains [41, 61, 82], the presented software prototypes contain separate modules for organizing the evolution of the DSL without the need for manual changes in the various levels of the DSL structure. At the same time, the created DSL dialects retain compatibility with the previously defined ones, as the changes are not only made at the level of specific DSL syntax but are transferred, using the cross-model transformation rules proposed by the authors, to the levels of abstract DSL syntax and DSM. In this way, complete coherence of evolution at all levels of DSL and DSM is ensured.

To achieve these results, formal mathematical methods were used, such as elements of function theory (Sect. 3.4) to formalize the relationship between the MCU and the MCC and implement cross-model transformations and elements of graph theory (Sects. 2.4, 3.4 and 3.5) to formalize the transformations between the DSL models and DSM.

The projection approach proposed in this paper differs significantly from the classical approach [83, 91], in which the DSM is considered only as a basis for the development of the DSL and is not used as an artefact in the DSL implementation process. In the case of the proposed approach, however, the development of the DSL is carried out sequentially, starting from the definition of the DSM with subsequent transformation through cross-model transformations into the semantic model (metamodel) of the DSL and transformation to the level of specific syntax with subsequent definition of individual commands in the case of textual DSL. Based on the ideas of cross-model transformations and object representation of the models used, the approach guarantees consistency of all levels of the DSL with the DSM, since the formal transformation mechanisms are based on graph transformations with preservation of the essential characteristics (properties) of the models.

In addition, a distinctive feature of the approach is the use of ontologies. If in existing works [83, 91] ontologies were used only as a basis for representing the DSL, without subsequent formal use in the design of the DSL, then in the proposed approach, the ontology is a full-fledged artifact (DSM) that determines the entire subsequent process of developing the DSL.

This use of ontologies makes it possible to organize a coordinated evolution of DSL dialects on the basis of a single DSM. This is achieved through the use of a system of consistent cross-model transformations, as well as an automated check of constraints derived from transformations and based on invariant mechanisms.

The effectiveness and flexibility of the proposed approach are demonstrated through the use of two different general-purpose software systems in the development process. It is important to note that the approach is universal and applies to both visual and textual types of DSLs for software systems, as demonstrated in the situations under consideration.

The approach, models, and methods proposed in this paper can be applied to the construction of general-purpose adaptive systems. However, it is not recommended for high-load, high-performance, demanding systems, where it is important to ensure a high level of security and system performance in the case of a large number of simultaneous users and requests.

The implementation of software for two different subject areas has resulted in the identification of reusable data structures and cross-model transformation algorithms to support the evolution of DSLs. This forms the basis for the development of general-purpose tools.

In the future, a possible extension of the approach could be the implementation of a full-fledged universal environment for DSL development (following the examples of MetaEdit+ [73] and ADOxx [117]), allowing not only to modify the set of created DSL constructions but also to support the organization of evolution of any DSL created by the tools of the environment.

We also plan to expand the functionality of using existing ontologies, which will allow us to organize bidirectional transformations in the structure of a DSL, thereby organizing not only the transition from DSM to DSL dialects but also the reverse one, replenishing the ontology with new concepts specified by users in the process of working with a DSL.

Appendix A
Example of an MCC Handler for an int Field MCU

```
...
public class IntInputPatternController {

    ...
    @FXML private TextField fieldData;
    @FXML private Text nameOfField;

    public String getFieldData() {
        if (checkData() != 0)
            return "";
        else {
            return fieldData.getText();
        }
    }

    public void setFieldData(String data) {
            fieldData.setText(data);
    }

    public void setParameters(String originalNameOfField,
    String nameOfField) {
        this.fieldOriginalName = originalNameOfField;
        this.nameOfField.setText(nameOfField);
    }

    public void setWidthHeight(Double paneWidth,
    Double paneHeight, Double labelWidth) {
        this.flowPane.setPrefWidth(paneWidth);
        this.flowPane.setPrefHeight(paneHeight);
        this.nameOfField.setWrappingWidth(labelWidth);
        this.fieldData.setPrefWidth(paneWidth -
        labelWidth - 40.0);
        this.fieldData.setPrefHeight(paneHeight*0.714);
    }
```

E. Babkin, B. Ulitin, *Ontology-Based Evolution of Domain-Oriented Languages*,
https://doi.org/10.1007/978-3-031-42202-7

```
public void setEditable(Boolean editChoice) {
    this.fieldData.setDisable(!editChoice);
}

public int checkData(){
    if(fieldData.getText().trim().isEmpty())
        return 1;
    if(Pattern.compile("(?!0)\\d+").matcher(
    fieldData.getText()).matches() ||
    Pattern.compile("(0)").matcher(
    fieldData.getText()).matches())
        return 0;
    else return 2;
}

}
```

Appendix B
Object-Relational Model MCU Correspondence Function and DSL MCC

```
...
for (int i = 0; i < countFields; i++) {
    switch (fieldsTypes[i]) {
        case "date":
            loader = new FXMLLoader();
            loader.setLocation(getClass().
            getResource(
            "./patterns_simple/DateInputPattern.fxml"
            ));

            newPane = (Pane) loader.load();
            fieldsControllers[i] = loader;

            childGridPane.add(newPane,2,0);
            DateInputPatternController
            dateInputPatternController =
            loader.getController();
            dateInputPatternController.setParameters(
            fields[i],
            ModelDBConnection.getTranslationOfField(
            fields[i], "AbiturientPassport");
            break;

        case "int":
            if(Pattern.compile("(id_t).*").matcher(
            fields[i]).matches() ){
                loader = new FXMLLoader();
                loader.setLocation(getClass().getResource(
                "./patterns_simple/ChoiceInputPattern.fxml"
                ));

                newPane = (Pane) loader.load();
                fieldsControllers[i] = loader;
```

```
            parentGridPane . add ( newPane , 0 , 0 );
            ChoiceInputPatternController
            choiceInputPatternController =
            loader . getController ();

            choiceInputPatternController . setParameters (
            fields [ i ],
            ModelDBConnection . getTranslationOfField (
            fields [ i ], " AbiturientPassport ");
            choiceInputPatternController .
            setFieldData ( "" );
            break ;
            }
            break ;

    case " varchar ":
        if ( Pattern . compile ( "( series ). * "). matcher (
        fields [ i ]). matches ()  ){
            loader = new FXMLLoader ();
            loader . setLocation ( getClass (). getResource (
            "./ patterns_simple / TextInputPattern . fxml "
            ));

            newPane = ( Pane ) loader . load ();
            fieldsControllers [ i ] = loader ;

            childGridPane . add ( newPane , 0 , 0 );
            TextInputPatternController
            textInputPatternController =
            loader . getController ();
            textInputPatternController . setParameters (
            fields [ i ],
            ModelDBConnection . getTranslationOfField (
            fields [ i ], " AbiturientPassport ");
            break ;
        }
    ...
    break ;
    }
}
...
```

Appendix C
Cross-Model Transformations in ATL

```
rule OWLClass2DSLClass {
    from a: OWL!OWLClass (does not exist (select b|
        b.isTypeOf (DSL!DSLClass) and a.name = b.name))
    to b: DSL!DSLClass,
        c:DSL!Constructor
}

rule DropDeletedOWLClassInDSLClass {
    from b: DSL! DSL Class (does not exist (select a|
        a.isTypeOf (OWL!OWLClass) and a.name = b.name))
    to drop do {
        drop c: DSL!Constructor (c.name = b.name) }
}

rule OWLClassAttributes2DSLClassAttributes {
    from a: OWL!OWLClass!OWLObjectProperty (
        does not exist (select b|
        b.isTypeOf (DSL!DSLClass!DSLObjectProperty)
        and a.name = b.name))
    to b: DSL!DSLClass!DSLObjectProperty (
        b.owner.name = a.owner.name),
        c: DSL!Constructor!DSLObjectProperty (
        b.owner.name = c.owner.name)
}

rule DropDeletedOWLClassAttributesInDSLClassAttributes
{
    from b: DSL!DSLClass!DSLObjectProperty (
        not exist (select a|
            a.isTypeOf (OWL!OWLClass!OWLObjectProperty
        ) and a.name = b.name))
    to drop
    do {
        drop c: DSL!Constructor!DSLObjectProperty (
        c.name = b.name) }
```

© The Author(s), under exclusive license to Springer Nature Switzerland AG 2024
E. Babkin, B. Ulitin, *Ontology-Based Evolution of Domain-Oriented Languages*,
https://doi.org/10.1007/978-3-031-42202-7

```
}

rule  OWLClassWithParents2DSLClassWithParents {
    from  a:  OWL!OWLClass  (a.parent −>exists())
    to  b:  DSL!DSLClass  (b.name = a.name),
        do { b.parent.name = a.parent.name }
}

rule  DropDeletedOWLClassParentsInDSLClasses {
    from  b:  DSL!DSLClass (
        not  exist  (select a|
            a.isTypeOf  (OWL!OWLClass)
            and a.name = b.name and
            a.parent.name = b.parent.name))
    to  drop  b.parent
        do { drop  c:  DSL!Function!DSLObjectProperty(
            c−>getProperties()−>contains(b.parent))
        }
}
```

Appendix D
Textual DSL for Railway Station Resource Allocation

```
Trains ({
    id
    type
    priority
    length
    timearrival timeDeparture
    timeReserve [ services ]
    wagonsToService })*
EndTrainsBlock;

Services ({
    fname
    priority
    mayBeInParallel [skills]
    standartDuration timeReserve
    [ equipment ] })*
endServiceBlock;

Brigades ({
    fid
    [ skills ]
    capacity })*
endBrigadeBlock;

Railways ({
    fid
    type
    totalLength usefulLength
    [ equipment ] })*
endRailwayBlock;

Appointments ({
    idBrigade->idTrain
    timestart timeEnd })*
endappointmentBlock;
```

```
Allocation ({
    idTrain->idRailway
    startNick timeStartOccupation
    timeEndOccupation }) *
endAllocationBlock;
```

Relocate idTrain [from idOldRailway] to idNewRailway;
/*This command allows to move Train with identifier idTrain
from railway with identifier idOldRailway to railway
idNewRailway.*/

Move forward/back idTrain by countShifts;
/*This command allows to move Train within current railway
forward or back by count of shifts equals to countShifts.*/

Put idTrain on newStartNick;
/*This command places the train with identifier idTrain
on start nick with number newStartNick.*/

ChangePriority idTrain/nameService on newPriority;
/*This command allows to change priority of train or service
on some new value newPriority.*/

Appoint idBrigade on idTrain from startTime [to endTime]
perform nameService;
/*This command allows to appoint brigade with identifier
idBrigade for servicing nameService on Train idTrain
within the period from startTime to endTime.*/

Get info on brigade/train/service/railway idEntity;
/*This command returns all the attributes for
brigade, train, service or railway identified by idEntity.*/

Glossary

Abstract DSL syntax (metamodel)   is an artefact that describes the concepts (objects) of a language, the relationships between them, and, optionally, constraints on the combination of concepts to comply with the rules of the subject domain [14].

Concrete DSL syntax (notation)   is an artefact that describes the rules for mapping an abstract DSL syntax to a text or graphical representation [18].

Domain-specific language (DSL)   a computer language (including programming or modelling) with limited expressive power, oriented towards a specific subject area [36].

Domain semantic model (DSM)   is an information model of a subject domain containing a set of domain concepts (terms) and the relationships between them [14].

DSL semantics   is a set of rules for interpreting (mapping) an abstract DSL syntax in terms of a formal (semantic) model of the target domain [41].

Dynamic context   represents and takes into account those aspects of the environment regarding the software solution (language as a whole) that may lead to the need to make changes (adaptations) over time or during an ongoing evaluation, and without which the software solution (language as a whole) cannot be used [25].

External DSL   a DSL separated from the main application language (general-purpose language) with which it operates. It can be either visual or text based [36].

Internal DSL   a DSL that is a specific way of using a general-purpose language and is written in the language of the main application [36].

Ontology   is a representational artefact containing a conceptual representation of a domain in the form of a set of classes (concepts) and the relationships between them with a corresponding set of constraints [43, 44]. It can be used as DSM.

Textual DSL   a DSL whose specific syntax is represented in textual form [61].

Visual DSL   a DSL whose specific syntax is represented graphically [54].

E. Babkin, B. Ulitin, *Ontology-Based Evolution of Domain-Oriented Languages*,
https://doi.org/10.1007/978-3-031-42202-7

References

1. Agrawal, A., Karsai, G., Shi, F.: Graph transformations on domain-specific models. Int. J. Softw. Syst. Model., 1–43 (2003)
2. Akehurst, D., Kent, S.: A relational approach to defining transformations in a metamodel. In: J.-M. Jézéquel, H. Hussmann, S. Cook (eds.), Proc. Fifth International Conference on the Unified Modeling Language – The Language and Its Applications, LNCS, pp. 243–258. Springer, Heidelberg (2002)
3. Amrani, M., Lucio, L., Selim, G., Combemale, B., Dingel, J., Vangheluwe, H., Traon, Y.L., Cordy, J.: A tridimensional approach for studying the formal verification of model transformations. Verification and validation of model Transformations (VOLT) (2012)
4. ANother Tool for Language Recognition (ANTLR): Available via DIALOG (2023). http://www.antlr.org/. Cited 10 Apr 2023
5. Anureev, I.S.: Domain-oriented navigation systems: object model and language. Syst. Inf. **1**, 1–34 (2013)
6. Arp, R., Smith, B., Spear, A.D.: Building Ontologies with Basic Formal Ontology. The MIT Press, Cambridge (2015)
7. ATL Transformation Language: Available via DIALOG (2023). http://www.eclipse.org/atl/. Cited 10 Apr 2023
8. Bacchus, F., Beek, P.V.: On the conversion between non-binary and binary constraint satisfaction problems. In: Proceedings of the 15th National Conference on Artificial Intelligence (AAAI-98) and of the 10th Conference on Innovative Applications of Artificial Intelligence (IAAI-98), pp. 311-318 (1998)
9. Bashir, R.S., Lee, S.P., Khan, S.U.R., Chang, V., Farid, S.: UML models consistency management: Guidelines for software quality manager. Int. J. Inf. Manag. **36**(6), 883–899 (2016)
10. Bell, P.: Automated transformation of statements within evolving domain specific languages. Comput. Sci. Inf. Syst. Rep., 172–177 (2007)
11. Belozerova, I.G., Nesvetova, E.A.: Research of Operations at Railway Stations. DVGUPS, Khabarovsk (2012)
12. Belozerova, I.G., Nesvetova, E.A.: Operational Management of the Station. DVGUPS, Khabarovsk (2012)
13. Bergmann, G., Ráth, I., Varró, G., Varró, D.: Change-driven model transformations. Soft. Syst. Model. **11**(3), 431–461 (2021)
14. Bezivin, J.: On the unification power of models. J. Softw. Syst. Model. **4**(2), 171–188 (2005)
15. Binmore, K.: Rational Decisions. Princeton University Press, Princeton (2009)

16. Bondavalli, A., Dal Cin, M., Latella, D., Majzik, I., Pataricza, A., Savoia, G.: Dependability analysis in the early phases of UML based system design. Int. J. Comput. Syst. Sci. Eng. **16**(5), 265–275 (2001)

17. Bulonkov, M.A., Ershov, A.P.: How special translation constructions can be generated by universal processes of mixed computing. Andrey Petrovich Ershov – scientist and man: collection, 101–120 (2006)

18. Cabot, J., Clarisó, R., Guerra, E., de Lara, J.: Verification and validation of declarative model-to-model transformations through invariants. J. Syst. Softw. **83**(2), 283–302 (2010)

19. Challenger, M., Demirkol, S., Getir, S., Mernik, M., Kardas, G., Kosar, T.: On the use of a domain-specific modeling language in the development of multiagent systems. Eng. Appl. Artif. Intell., 111–141 (2014)

20. Chandy, K.M., Mani, K., Misra, J.: Parallel Program Design: A Foundation. Addison-Wesley, Boston (1998)

21. Charter of the Railway Transport: Federal Law of January 10, 2003 N 18-FZ (2003) Available via DIALOG. https://cis-legislation.com/document.fwx?rgn=3580. Cited 10 Apr 2023

22. Chen, W., Dong, M.: Optimal resource allocation across related channels. Oper. Res. Lett., 397–401 (2018)

23. Choco Solver: Available via DIALOG (2023). http://choco-solver.org/. Cited 10 Apr 2023

24. Cleenewerck, T.: Component-based DSL development. Softw. Lang. Eng., 245–264 (2003)

25. Cleenewerck, T., Czarnecki, K., Striegnitz, J., Volter, M.: Evolution and Reuse of Language Specifications for DSLs (ERLS). Object-Oriented Technology. ECOOP 2004 Workshop Reader, 187–201 (2004)

26. Degrandsart, S., Demeyer, S., Van den Bergh, J., Mens, T.: A transformation-based approach to context-aware modelling. Softw. Syst. Model. **13**(1), 191–208 (2014)

27. Demuth, A., Riedl-Ehrenleitner, M., Lopez-Herrejon, R.E., Egyed, A.: Co-evolution of metamodels and models through consistent change propagation. J. Syst. Softw., 281–297 (2016)

28. Disolver: Available via DIALOG (2023). http://research.microsoft.com/apps/pubs/default.aspx?id=64335. Cited 10 Apr 2023

29. Eclipse Graphical Modeling Project (GMP): Available via DIALOG (2023). http://www.eclipse.org/modeling/gmp/. Cited 10 Apr 2023

30. Ehrig, H., Ehrig, K., Prange, U., Taentzer, G.: Fundamentals of Algebraic Graph Transformation. Enschede, The Netherlands (2006)

31. Eisenberg, C.: Distributed Constraint Satisfaction for Coordinating and Integrating a Large-Scale, Heterogeneous Enterprise. University of London, London (2013)

32. Ershov, A.P.: A denotational approach to describing transformational semantics. Presentation slides at the CIP project seminar at the Technical University of Munich (1982)

33. Evans, E.: Domain-Driven Design: Tackling Complexity in the Heart of Software. Addison-Wesley, Boston (2013)

34. Fedorenkov, V.G., Balakshin, P.V.: CFeatures of the use of domain-specific languages for testing web applications. Softw. Prod. Syst. **4**, 601–606 (2019)

35. Fernandez-Lopez, M., Gomez-Perez, A.: Overview and analysis of methodologies for building ontologies. Knowl. Eng. Rev., 129–156 (2002)

36. Fowler, M.: Domain Specific Languages. Addison-Wesley, Boston (2010)

37. Gecode Toolkit: Available via DIALOG (2023). http://www.gecode.org/. Cited 10 Apr 2023

38. Giese, H., Hildebrandt, S., Lambers, L.: Bridging the gap between formal semantics and implementation of triple graph grammars. Softw. Syst. Model. **13**, 273–299 (2014)

39. Gogolla, M., Bohling, J., Richters, M.: Validating UML and OCL models in USE by automatic snapshot generation. J. Softw. Syst. Model. **4**(4), 386–398 (2005)

40. Golobisky, M.F., Vecchietti, A.: Mapping UML class diagrams into object-relational schemas. In: Proceedings of Argentine Symposium on Software Engineering, pp. 65–79 (2005)

41. Gómez-Abajo, P., Guerra, E., de Lara, J.: A domain-specific language for model mutation and its application to the automated generation of exercises. Comput. Lang. Syst. Struct. **49**, 152–173 (2016)

42. GReAT: Graph Rewriting and Transformation. Available via DIALOG (2023). http://www.isis.vanderbilt.edu/tools/great. Cited 10 Apr 2023
43. Guizzardi, G.: Ontological Foundations for Structural Conceptual Models. Enschede, The Netherlands (2005)
44. Guizzardi, G., Halpin, T.: Ontological foundations for conceptual modeling. Appl. Ontol. **3**, 91–110 (2008)
45. Gaifullin, B.N., Tumanov, V.E.: Subject-oriented systems of scientific awareness in science and education. Modern Inf. Technol. IT Educ. **8**, 741–750 (2012)
46. GOST R ISO/IEC 12207-2010: SYSTEM AND SOFTWARE ENGINEERING Software Life Cycle Processes (2012) Available via DIALOG. https://docs.cntd.ru/document/1200082859. Cited 10 Apr 2023
47. GOST R ISO/IEC 25010-2015: SYSTEM AND SOFTWARE ENGINEERING Requirements and quality assessment of systems and software (SQuaRE). Quality models of systems and software products (2015) Available via DIALOG. https://docs.cntd.ru/document/1200121069. Cited 10 Apr 2023
48. Haav, H.-M., Ojamaa, A., Grigorenko, P., Kotkas, V.: Ontology-based integration of software artefacts for DSL development. On the move to meaningful internet systems: OTM 2015 workshops. Lect. Notes Comput. Sci. **9416**, 309–318 (2015)
49. Hausmann, J.H., Heckel, R., Sauer, S.: Extended model relations with graphical consistency conditions. In: UML 2002 Workshop on Consistency Problems in UML-based Software Development, pp. 61–74 (2002)
50. Hayat, S.A.E., Toufik, F., Bahaj, M.: UML/OCL based design and the transition towards temporal object relational database with bitemporal data. J. King Saud Univ. Comput. Inf. Sci. **32**(4), 398–407 (2020)
51. Heavin, C., Power, D.J.: Challenges for digital transformation – towards a conceptual decision support guide for managers. J. Decis. Syst. **27**(1), 38–45 (2018)
52. Hodgson, M.: On the limits of rational choice theory. Economic Thought, 94–108 (2012)
53. JastAdd: Available via DIALOG (2023). https://jastadd.cs.lth.se/web/. Cited 10 Apr 2023
54. Kelly, S., Tolvanen J.-P.: Domain-Specific Modeling: Enabling Full Code Generation. Wiley-IEEE ComputerSociety Press, Hoboken, New Jersey, USA (2008)
55. Kessentini, W., Sahraoui, H., Wimmer, M.: Automated metamodel/model co-evolution: A search-based approach. Inf. Softw. Technol., 49–67 (2019)
56. Khelladi, D.E., Bendraou, R., Hebig, R., Gervais, M.-P.: A semi-automatic maintenance and co-evolution of OCL constraints with (meta)model evolution. J. Syst. Softw., 242–260 (2017)
57. Köhler, H., Link, S.: SQL schema design: foundations, normal forms, and normalization. Inf. Syst. **76**, 88–113 (2018)
58. Königs, A., Schürr, A.: Tool integration with triple graph grammars - a survey. ENTCS **148**, 113–150 (2006)
59. Kogalovsky M.R., Kalinichenko L.A.: Conceptual and ontological modeling in information systems. Programming **35**(5), 241–256 (2009)
60. Konyrbaev, N.B., Ibadulla, S.I., Diveev, A.I.: Evolutional methods for creating artificial intelligence of robotic technical systems. Procedia Comput. Sci. **150**, 709–715 (2019)
61. Kosar, T., Bohra, B., Mernik, M.: Domain-specific languages: a systematic mapping study. Inf. Softw. Technol., 77–90 (2016)
62. Kosar, T., Martínez Lopez, P., Barrientos, P., Mernik, M.: A preliminary study on various implementation approaches of domain-specific language. Inf. Softw. Technol., 390–405 (2008)
63. Küster, J.M., Abd-El-Razik, M.: Validation of model transformations – first experiences using a white box approach. In: Kühne, T. (ed.) MoDELS Workshops, LNCS, pp. 193–204. Springer, Heidelberg (2006)
64. Laird, P., Barrett, S.: Towards dynamic evolution of domain specific languages. Softw. Lang. Eng., 144–153 (2010)
65. Lazareva, O.F., McInnerney, J., Williams, T.: Implicit relational learning in a multiple-object tracking task. Behav. Process. **152**, 26–36 (2018)

66. Leung, Y.: Artificial intelligence and expert systems. Int. Encyclopedia Hum. Geogr. (Second Edition), 209–215 (2020)
67. Lucassen, G., Robeer, M., Dalpiaz, F., Werf, G.M., Brinkkemper, S.: Extracting conceptual models from user stories with Visual Narrator. Requir. Eng. **22**(3), 339–358 (2017)
68. Luoma, J., Kelly, S., Tolvanen, J.-P.: Defining domain-specific modeling languages: Collected experiences. In: Proceedings of the 4th OOPSLA Workshop on Domain-Specific Modeling (DSM'04) (2004)
69. Mengerink, J.G.M., Serebrenik, A., van den Brand, M., Schiffelers, R.R.H.: Udapt Edapt Extensions for Industrial Application. In: ITSLE 2016 Industry Track for Software Language Engineering October 31, 2016, Amsterdam, Netherlands, 21–22 (2016)
70. Mengerink, J.G.M., Serebrenik, A., Schiffelers, R.R.H., van den Brand, M.: A complete operator library for DSL evolution specification. In: MDSE 32nd International Conference on Software Maintenance and Evolution, pp. 144–154 (2016)
71. Mens, T., Czarnecki, K., Gorp, P.V.: A taxonomy of model transformations. Electron. Notes Theor. Comput. Sci. **152**, 125–142 (2006)
72. Mernik, M., Heering, J., Sloane, A.: When and how to develop domain-specific languages. ACM Comput. Surv. (CSUR) **37**(4), 316–344 (2005)
73. MetaCase+: Available via DIALOG (2023). http://www.metacase.com/. Cited 10 Apr 2023
74. MetaLanguage: Available via DIALOG (2023). http://pespmc1.vub.ac.be/METALARE.html. Cited 10 Apr 2023
75. Milne, C., Strachey, R.: A Theory of Programming Language Semantics (2 Vol). Chapman and Hall, London (1976)
76. Mohagheghi, P., Haugen, Ø.: Evaluating Domain-Specific Modelling Solutions. In: ER 2010 Workshops, pp. 212–221 (2010)
77. Nonaka, I., Kodama, M., Hirose, A., Kohlbacher, F.: Dynamic fractal organizations for promoting knowledge-based transformation—A new paradigm for organizational theory. Eur. Manag. J. **32**(1), 137–146 (2014)
78. Nabiullin, O.R., Babkin, E.A.: Modeling and automatic verification by AsmL. Bus. Inf. **4**, 56–63 (2008)
79. Nabiullin, O.R., Norkin, V.M.: Architecture of a high-performance multi-agent modeling system. Bus. Inf. **2**, 48–60 (2008)
80. On Information, Information Technologies and Information Protection: Federal Law of July 27, 2006 No.149-FZ. Available via DIALOG (2021). https://eais.rkn.gov.ru/docs.eng/149.pdf. Cited 10 Apr 2023
81. On the approval of the classifier of programs for electronic computers and databases: Order of the Ministry of Digital Development, Telecommunications and Mass Media No. 486. Available via DIALOG (2021). https://digital.gov.ru/en/. Cited 10 Apr 2023
82. Parr, T.: Language Implementation Patterns: Create Your Own Domain-Specific and General Programming Languages. Pragmatic Bookshelf, Raleigh, NC (2012)
83. Pereira, M.J.V., Fonseca, J., Henriques, P.R.: Ontological approach for DSL development. Comput. Lang. Syst. Struct. **45**, 35–52 (2016)
84. Polyglot: Available via DIALOG (2023). https://www.cs.cornell.edu/projects/polyglot/. Cited 10 Apr 2023
85. Popovic, A., Lukovic, I., Dimitrieski, V., Djuki, V.: DSL for modeling application-specific functionalities of business applications. Comput. Lang. Syst. Struct., 69–95 (2015)
86. Prud'homme, C., Lorca, X., Douence, R., Jussien, N.: Propagation engine prototyping with a domain specific language. Constraints, 57–77 (2013)
87. QVT (Query/View/Transformation): Available via DIALOG (2023). https://projects.eclipse.org/projects/modeling.mmt.qvt-oml. Cited 10 Apr 2023
88. Rahim, L.A., Whittle, J.: A survey of approaches for verifying model transformations. Softw. Syst. Model. **14**(2), 1003–1028 (2015)
89. Ruffolo, M., Sidhu, I., Guadagno, L.: Semantic Enterprise Technologies. In: Proceedings of the First International Conference on Industrial Results of Semantic Technologies, vol. 293, pp. 70–84 (2007)

90. Sanders, B.A.: Eliminating the substitution axiom from UNITY logic. Form. Asp. Comput. **3**, 189–205 (1991)
91. Schürr, A.: Graph-transformation-driven correct-by-construction development of communication system topology adaptation algorithms. In: Schaefer, I., Karagiannis, D., Vogelsang, A., Méndez, D., Seidl, C. (eds.) Modellierung, LNI, pp. 15–29. Springer, Heidelberg (2018)
92. Shcherbina, O.: Nonserial dynamic programming and tree decomposition in discrete optimization. In: Proceedings of Int. Conference on Operations Research, pp. 155–160 (2007)
93. SPIN Model Checker: Available via DIALOG (2023). http://spinroot.com/spin/whatispin. html. Cited 10 Apr 2023
94. Sprinkle, J.: A domain-specific visual language for domain model evolution. J. Visual Lang. Comput., 291–307 (2004)
95. Sprinkle, J.: A safe autonomous vehicle trajectory domain specific modelling language for non-expert development. In: Proceedings of the International Workshop on Domain-Specific Modeling, pp. 42–48 (2016)
96. SQL Standard 2016 (ISO/IEC 9075-1:2016): Available via DIALOG (2023). https://www. iso.org/committee/45342/x/catalogue/p/1/u/0/w/0/d/0. Cited 10 Apr 2023
97. Stoy, J.E.: Denotational Semantics: The Scott-Strachey Approach to Programming Language Theory. MIT Press, Cambridge (1985)
98. Sukhov, A.O.: Classification of domain-specific languages and language tools. Math. Program Syst. 74–83 (2012)
99. Tereshina, N.P.: Economics of railway transport: a textbook. FGBOU "Educational and methodological center for education in railway transport" (2012)
100. Torres, A., Galante, R., Pimenta, M.S., Martins, A.J.B.: Twenty years of object-relational mapping: A survey on patterns, solutions, and their implications on application design. Inf. Softw. Technol. **82**, 1–18 (2017)
101. Ulitin, B., Babkin, E., Babkina, T.: Combination of DSL and DCSP for decision support in dynamic contexts. In: Lecture Notes in Business Information Processing Issue 261: Perspectives in Business Informatics Research, pp. 159–173 (2016)
102. Ulitin, B., Babkin, E.: Ontology and DSL co-evolution using graph transformations methods. In: Lecture Notes in Business Information Processing Issue 295: Perspectives in Business Informatics Research, pp. 233–247 (2017)
103. Ulitin, B., Babkin, E., Babkina, T.: A projection-based approach for development of domain-specific languages. In: Lecture Notes in Business Information Processing Issue 330: Perspectives in Business Informatics Research, pp. 219–234 (2018)
104. Ulitin, B., Babkin, E., Babkina, T., Vizgunov, A.: Automated formal verification of model transformations using the invariants mechanism. In: Lecture Notes in Business Information Processing Issue 365: Perspectives in Business Informatics Research, pp. 59–73 (2018)
105. Ulitin, B., Babkin, E.: Ontology-based reconfigurable DSL for planning technical services. IFAC-PapersOnLine **52**(13), 1138–1144 (2019)
106. Ulitin, B., Babkin, E.: Providing models of DSL evolution using model-to-model transformations and invariants mechanisms. In: Digital Transformation and New Challenges, Lecture Notes in Information Systems and Organisation, vol. 40, pp. 37–48 (2020)
107. Ulsamer, P., Fertig, T., Braun, P.: Feature-oriented domain-specific languages. In: Dagstuhl Workshop MBEES: Modellbasierte Entwicklung eingebetteter Systeme XIV, Schloss Dagstuhl, Germany, 2018, Tagungsband Modellbasierte Entwicklung eingebetteter Systeme, pp. 31–40 (2018)
108. Varró, D., Varró-Gyapay, S., Ehrig, H., Prange, U., Taentzer, G.: Termination analysis of model transformations by petri nets. In: Graph Transformations, Lecture Notes in Computer Science, vol. 4178, pp. 260–274 (2006)
109. Viatra Eclipse: Available via DIALOG (2023). https://www.eclipse.org/viatra/. Cited 10 Apr 2023
110. Wang, N., Wang, D., Zhang, Y.: Design of an adaptive examination system based on artificial intelligence recognition model. Mech. Syst. Signal Process. **142**, 1–14 (2020)

111. Wang, N., Wang, D., Zhang, Y.: Dynamic resource allocation for intermodal freight transportation with network effects: Approximations and algorithms. Transp. Res. B Methodol., 83–112 (2017)
112. Wu, Y., Mu, T., Liatsis, P., Goulermas, J.Y.: Computation of heterogeneous object co-embeddings from relational measurements. Pattern Recognit. **65**, 146–163 (2017)
113. XText Eclipse: Available via DIALOG (2023). https://www.eclipse.org/Xtext/. Cited 10 Apr 2023
114. Yokoo, M.: Distributed Constraint Satisfaction. Springer, New York (2001)
115. Zakharov, V.N., Kalinichenko, L.A., Sokolov, I.A., Stupnikov, S.A.: Designing canonical information models for integrated information systems. Inf. Appl. **1**(2), 15–38 (2007)
116. Zhang, Y., Xu, B.: A survey of semantic description frameworks for programming languages. SIGPLAN Not. **39**(3), 14–30 (2004)
117. Zipped ADOxx: Available via DIALOG (2023). https://www.adoxx.org/live/home. Cited 10 May 2023

Printed in the United States
by Baker & Taylor Publisher Services